Guantánamo North

D0860808

Guantánamo North

Terrorism and the
Administration of Justice in Canada

Robert Diab

Fernwood Publishing • Halifax & Winnipeg

Editing: Eileen Young
Cover Design: John van der Woude
Printed and bound in Canada by Hignell Book Printing

Published in Canada by Fernwood Publishing
Site 2A, Box 5, 32 Oceanvista Lane
Black Point, Nova Scotia, B0J 1B0
and #8 - 222 Osborne Street, Winnipeg, Manitoba, R3L 1Z3
www.fernwoodpublishing.ca

Fernwood Publishing Company Limited gratefully acknowledges the financial support
of the Government of Canada through the Book Publishing Industry Development
Program (BPDIP), the Canada Council for the Arts and the Nova Scotia
Department of Tourism and Culture for our publishing program.

Library and Archives Canada Cataloguing in Publication

Diab, Robert
Guantánamo north: terrorism and the administration of justice in
Canada / Robet Diab.

ISBN 978-1-55266-281-6

1. Terrorism--Prevention--Government policy--Canada. 2. National
security--Law and legislation--Canada. 3. Terrorism--Canada--Prevention.
4. Civil rights--Canada. 5. Justice, Administration of--Canada. I. Title.

KE9007.D52 2008   345.71'02   C2008-903344-2
KF9430.D52 2008

Contents

Acknowledgements

I would like to thank W. Wesley Pue for encouraging me to continue with a project that began as an LL.M. thesis at the Faculty of Law at the University of British Columbia, and for helping along the way by offering many invaluable editorial suggestions. Without his enthusiasm and inspiration, this book would not have been written.

I am also indebted to Wayne Antony at Fernwood Publishing for his keen insight and helpful guidance on how to develop the arguments and material in this book, and to Steve Brittle, whose critique of an earlier version of the text provoked me to rethink substantial portions of it. My thanks also to Eileen Young for copy editing; Beverley Rach for the layout and design; John van der Woude for cover design; Debbie Mathers for editing input; and Brenda Conroy for proofreading.

Many thanks also to Professor Robin Elliot, Q.C., for graciously agreeing to act as my supervisor at UBC, for many provocative and memorable conversations about constitutional law and other matters, and for suggestions on the present text. I would also wish to thank Kent Roach, who was kind enough to provide comments on an earlier draft.

Finally, this project would not have been possible without the generous support, love, and encouragement of my wife, Ciara, who bore many burdens to give me the time to work and provided extremely helpful comments on the text.

List of Acronyms

APEC — the Asia-Pacific Economic Cooperation, an inter-governmental association that meets periodically to discuss trade and development issues.

ATA — the *Anti-Terrorism Act*.

CPC — the Commission for Public Complaints Against the RCMP, an independent agency mandated by Parliament to investigate public complaints about the conduct of members of the RCMP.

CSE — the Communications Security Establishment, a national agency that provides the Government of Canada with assistance in the fields of cryptography (code-making and code-breaking) and foreign signals intelligence.

CAUT — the Canadian Association of University Teachers, an association that advocates on behalf of Canadian academics.

CSIS — the Canadian Security Intelligence Service, a national agency that investigates threats to national security and produces intelligence for the government of Canada.

FINTRAC — the Financial Transactions and Reports Analysis Centre of Canada, a national financial intelligence agency that collects and analyzes intelligence relating to suspected money laundering and terrorist activities.

ICRA — the Independent Complaints and National Security Review Agency, an entity proposed by the Arar Commission that would deal with the national security activities of the RCMP and related law enforcement agencies.

INSET — Integrated National Security Enforcement Teams consist of members of the RCMP, various national agencies, such as the Canada Border Services Agency and CSIS, and provincial and municipal police forces. They are mandated to collect and share information in national security investigations.

INSRCC — the Integrated National Security Review Coordinating Committee, an entity proposed by the Arar Commission that would review the national security activities of the ICRA, the CSE, and the SIRC.

IRPA — the *Immigration and Refugee Protection Act*.

NSID — the National Security Investigation Directorate, an entity within the RCMP that oversees national security investigations.

NSIS — National Security Investigation Sections, entities within the RCMP in which specific investigations were conducted; now replaced by INSETs.

NSOB — the National Security Operations Branch, an entity within the RCMP that monitors and directs national security investigations.

RCMP — the Royal Canadian Mounted Police, a national police force with a wide ranging law-enforcement mandate, including the prevention and investigation of terrorism offences.

SIRC — the Security Intelligence Review Committee, an independent review body that reports to Parliament on the activities of CSIS.

Introduction

Between May of 2000 and 2003, the Canadian government would order the arrest of five Muslim immigrants and hold them in custody for between two and seven years.[1] Their cases had become a matter of national interest primarily because of the unusual circumstances under which they had been held. They were each deemed to be a threat to national security, but none has been charged with a crime. None has been given the opportunity to hear all of the evidence against him. They were each excluded from attending some of the court hearings in their own cases. And since none of the men could be deported to their country of origin, for fear of torture, their detention in Canada was indefinite.

The government's case against what have come to be known as the "secret trial five" appears to consist mostly of circumstantial evidence. One man (Mohammed Mahjoub) had worked in Sudan at a farm owned by Osama bin Laden and had met the al-Qaeda leader a number of times.[2] He was also known to associate with a suspected terrorist residing in Canada and with others abroad: undisclosed information suggests it is likely that he was a member of the al-Jihad terrorist organization in Egypt as well as al-Qaeda. Another of the detainees was identified in a photograph shown to two convicted terrorists serving sentences in the United States: they claim to have recognized him from training camps in Afghanistan. (One later recanted.[3]) A third man is also believed to have been involved in al-Jihad: he had social links with a known terrorist in Canada and others abroad. He also placed a number of phone calls to persons believed to be linked to terrorism in various countries, and followed a "travel pattern" in the early 1990s that was "consistent with the profile of an Islamic Mujahadeen extremist."[4] In none of the five cases does the evidence amount to proof of a conspiracy to commit a terrorist act or proof of involvement in a past terrorist act. But

9

the evidence clearly suggests a possible threat to national security.

The question for those who make, apply, and enforce the law is how to respond to this threat without abandoning the ideals and principles that form the basis of our legal system. As the threat of terrorism has become more vivid and pervasive since September 11, 2001, we have become less inclined to think of people suspected of a link to terrorism as ordinary criminal suspects entitled to justice and fairness. Although we are committed to justice, the nature of the threat compels us to take extraordinary precautions. Many of these precautions may not be fair; some are altogether unjust.

Under the terms of criminal law, each of the men among the "secret trial five" would be presumed innocent until proven guilty. But in this case, it is almost the reverse. Out of an abundance of caution, we have proceeded to treat these men as guilty and to forgo the need to present evidence in a full trial. We have held them in an administrative limbo that is officially neither a detention pending deportation nor a punishment, but simply an indefinite incarceration. We have preferred to deal with these cases using the language of risk management rather than crime and punishment. However, as a society that prides itself on maintaining high standards of civil and human rights, and enjoying the protections of a constitutional *Canadian Charter of Rights and Freedoms*, we must at some point consider the possibility of their innocence. We must ask: what if even one of these men is innocent?

To begin to appreciate what can happen when a person is wrongfully accused of a link to terrorism, consider the case of Maher Arar. In 2002, Arar, a Syrian-born Canadian, was travelling home from a family vacation in Tunisia. He was an engineer and entrepreneur, and had lived in Canada since 1989. He had no criminal record. He was an otherwise ordinary Arab-Canadian. At a stopover in New York, American customs officials detained him, acting on information provided by the Royal Canadian Mounted Police (RCMP) that purported to link Arar to a terrorist suspect. (The information concerned Arar's fleeting encounter with the brother of an acquaintance in Ottawa. The brother, whom Arar hardly knew, happened to be a person of interest to Canadian authorities.) Arar was held in custody in the United States for twelve days, without being told why he was detained and without having access to a lawyer for nine days. He was deported to Jordan, where he was blind-folded, beaten and interrogated for a number of days, and then sent to a notoriously brutal Syrian prison, where he was tortured repeatedly, and held in a windowless, underground cell measuring three feet wide, six feet deep and seven feet high, for ten months and ten days. Under these circumstances, he agreed to any statement put to him and signed a number of false confessions. He was eventually transferred to another Syrian prison where he spent a night in a cell that measured six by four metres and held forty-six people. Canadian officials were slow to intervene on his behalf and did so largely in response to the relentless efforts of Arar's wife, Monia Mazigh, in Canada. Eventually, it became clear to Canadian officials that Arar was not a terrorist or a threat to national security; they then helped to secure his eventual release one year and nine days after his arrest (Arar 2008).

In each of these cases, the government has relied on secret intelligence, or information acquired by the Canadian Security and Intelligence Service (CSIS) or the RCMP, from a number of sources, including foreign governments or intelligence agencies. Intelligence may consist of hard evidence — documents, photographs, wiretaps — or it might consist of mere gossip, innuendo, suggestion, or outright fabrication by sources motivated to mislead authorities. In some cases, it might be based on statements compelled under torture.

In a conventional criminal case, the prosecution relies not on information that it may conceal from the accused or the public, but on evidence that it must disclose to the accused before the trial, and that it must then submit to the scrutiny of both the accused and the public in a "full and fair trial." At the least, this includes a hearing at which the accused is present and has a chance to examine the evidence, to question the prosecution's witnesses in an adverse fashion, and to call his or her own witnesses in rebuttal. The judge or jury, who remain impartial and independent throughout, weigh the evidence only after both the prosecution and the accused have had a chance to present competing theories of the case, based on a thorough assessment of all the evidence.

By contrast with the use of evidence in ordinary criminal cases, governments throughout the west have come to rely increasingly, since September 11th, on secret intelligence in counter-terrorism proceedings.[5] Therefore, in many of these cases, the credibility of the allegations cannot be fully tested. This has become a more serious problem as the government finds itself more frequently in the position of not having enough information to charge a person with an offence, but having enough to warrant extreme caution and extraordinary measures in dealing with them.

The "secret trial five" are the subject of one such extraordinary measure. They have been held under what are called "security certificates," which are provided for under the *Immigration and Refugee Protection Act* (2001).[6] Although the certificates have been a part of immigration law since the late 1970s, and the government had made occasional use of them before September 11th, they have since come to play a more important role in the government's response to terrorism. Under the Act, the Minister of Citizenship and Immigration and the Minister of Public Safety and Preparedness, together, can issue a certificate to detain a person who is not a citizen, where the ministers have a reasonable suspicion ("reasonable grounds to believe") that the person poses a threat to national security. A judge may review the detention, but the ministers can insist that the evidence in support of their position be disclosed only to the judge, while the detainee is given simply a "gist," or general idea, of the information against him or her. The judge decides only whether the decision to issue the certificate was reasonable, not whether the information in support of the ministers' position amounts to proof beyond a reasonable doubt.

"Administrative detention," as it is known, is only one of many extraordinary measures available to deal with suspected terrorists. In the fall of 2001, the Canadian government hastily drafted and passed the *Anti-Terrorism Act*,[7] which amended the criminal law, and a number of other statutes, to allow for "preventive arrests" and detentions without charge, to allow judges to conduct interrogations of persons who have not been charged with an offence, and to make "terrorism" itself an offence, with a definition so expansive that it includes motive as an element (something unusual in Canadian law) and allows for a conviction in a case where the offence itself is unknown to the accused, or is considered to be unintended. The Act also significantly expands government privilege in, and secrecy of, evidence in any proceeding in Canada, including a criminal trial.

The provisions allowing for preventive arrest and judicial interrogations lapsed in 2007, under the terms of a five-year sunset clause, but a bill currently before the Senate proposes to revive them. The definition of terrorism in the Act was challenged in the first prosecution under the Act: this resulted in the court striking down the motive element of the definition as unconstitutional, but upholding the constitutionality of the almost non-existent knowledge element in the offence.[8] (The Supreme Court of Canada declined to hear the appeal.)

The government will likely continue to make use of these tools in future cases involving terrorism: chief among them will be a set of provisions in the *Anti-Terrorism Act* that appear to be marginal or mostly technical in nature. These are sections amending the *Canada Evidence Act* to allow the government to assert privilege or maintain secrecy over a much broader scope of evidence than had previously been the case.[9] Before the amendment, the Act stated that evidence would be privileged only where "disclosure would be injurious to... international relations or national defence or security." It now states that evidence can be privileged if disclosure would be "potentially injurious."[10] Parliament has also added a new category of privilege over "sensitive information."[11] This includes any evidence relating to national security, defence or international relations that the government is "taking measures to safeguard." Moreover, the assertion of privilege is almost unreviewable.

The consequences of the government's power to operate with greater secrecy in administrative and criminal cases are far-reaching. Not only is it now possible to convict a person of a terrorist offence that he or she was not aware of, or did not intend to commit, it is possible to do so without fully disclosing the case against him or her. The expansion of state privilege also makes it more difficult to address any errors made on the part of the government or its investigators in the case of a wrongful conviction or accusation. Maher Arar's case is a good example. Soon after his return to Canada, the government ordered an inquiry into the events surrounding Arar's arrest and deportation. The Arar Inquiry had two purposes. One was to make findings of fact with respect to the incident. The other was to make recommendations that would help law enforcement, and the RCMP in particular, work more effectively and accountably in this context. The government's response to the Inquiry was to invoke the new secrecy provisions of the *Anti-Terrorism Act* to conceal much of the testimony of CSIS and RCMP personnel on their role in the incident, and to censor significant portions of the Inquiry's final report. Questions remain about the complicity of Canadian officials in Arar's torture and imprisonment in Syria. There are also broader concerns about whether the allegations in the security certificate cases, or other counter-terror investigations, have involved the use of information obtained abroad through torture.

A number of constitutional challenges to the *Anti-Terrorism Act* and the security certificate regime in the *Immigration and Refugee Protection Act* have been brought in response to these and other concerns. But in the vast majority of these cases, the Constitution, including the *Canadian Charter of Rights and Freedoms*, is proving to be of limited use. Among the most important of these challenges is a decision of the Supreme Court of Canada in an appeal brought in June of 2006 by three of the "secret trial five" dealing with the constitutional validity of the entire security certificate regime.[12] The appeal raised a number of concerns, including the use of secret evidence, hearings that would exclude the detainee, the possibility of indefinite detention, and the lack of a prohibition against evidence obtained by torture. In February of 2007, the Court ruled that the certificate regime violated the right to "life, liberty and security of the person" in section 7 of the *Canadian Charter of Rights and Freedoms*, and was not "in accordance with the principles of fundamental justice." The Court concluded, however, that the regime could be made consistent with the constitution if only a slight modification were made — allowing for the use of a "special advocate." A lawyer in this role would have access to secret evidence and argue on behalf of the detainee before the judge. Parliament has recently passed a bill amending the *Immigration and Refugee Protection Act* to allow for the use of special advocates, but ignoring many other outstanding concerns about the certificate regime.[13]

At the time of this writing, four of the men held under certificates have been released on bail, but each is subject to some of the most restrictive bail orders ever issued by a Canadian court. Each of the men is subject to house arrest and constant surveillance. In one case, the government is seeking permission to install video cameras in the detainee's apartment, which he shares with his family of six (Freeze 2007). The government still maintains privilege over evidence in each of the cases, and is appealing the decision to grant bail in the case of at least one of the detainees. The fifth detainee remains in custody indefinitely.

The certificate regime will likely remain an integral part of Canada's counter-terror strategy for some time to come, along with the new offences in the *Anti-Terrorism Act*, and the power of law enforcement and intelligence agencies to function with greater secrecy. Together, these developments have provoked a wide range of critical responses. Much of this commentary is, however, concerned primarily with the erosion of certain constitutional rights and principles, or the questionable expansion of the scope of our criminal law. But given the persistence of these developments in a system with so many constitutional protections, an analysis focused primarily on the letter of the law would seem incomplete at best.

Instead, I propose to assess the impact of Canada's response to terrorism on the administration of justice in a broader sense. I advance the argument that the legislative, judicial, and practical developments sketched above have created a deeper divide between the administration of justice and the theory and concepts that have served to guide it — and that to many of those involved, the divide appears to be unavoidable. To be clear, this is not a new divide: many of the more concerning developments discussed in this book have antecedents in the law, in one form or another, that pre-date September 11th. But as the threat of terrorism becomes more pervasive, and as the strategy for countering terrorism continues to shift ground from evidence gathering to secret intelligence, there is a greater impetus on the part of many lawmakers and enforcers to accept the growing divide between practice and principle within the administration of justice as an unfortunate but necessary consequence of the precautions that must be taken. I call the necessity for these precautions into question and suggest that the *Anti-Terrorism Act* should be repealed. In this way, the gap between practice and principle can begin to be closed.

My argument relies on reading the phrase, "the administration of justice," in two ways. I take it to refer to both the creation and enforcement of the law, but also to a host of concepts fundamental to our system of justice. A non-exhaustive list of these concepts would include due process, the independence and impartiality of the judiciary, the accountability of law enforcement and intelligence agencies, and perhaps most crucially, constitutionalism and the rule of law. I explore these concepts in more detail below. It is worth noting here, however, that the various agents involved in the legal system — police, prosecutors, defence counsel, judges, and lawmakers — do not subscribe to these concepts in a perfectly consistent manner, given that the roles they play are often contradictory or inconsistent in relation to one another. But collectively, these concepts are clearly central to the discourse that shapes the administration of justice in Canada.

The point of assessing the impact of terrorism on the administration of justice, and not only on constitutional rights per se, is to broaden the analysis to take into account the ways in which theory and practice diverge in this context, and to assess what impact this has on a whole range of stakeholders in the justice system. Elizabeth Comack and Gillian Balfour, in particular, take the view that the practice or application of the law has always functioned at a remove from the principles or ideology that guide it. From their perspective, the *Anti-Terrorism Act* and other measures explored in this book, can be understood as further examples of how the administration of justice, or the practice of law, deviates from principle or ideology.

In *Locating Law*, Comack seeks to understand the nature of this divide by adopting Ngaire Naffine's distinction between two ways of reading the law (Naffine 1990). In theory, the law is a system that is meant to be "fair, dispassionate, disinterested," and "just" (Comack 2006: 22). The law also asks us to assume that the subject of the law, or a person who enters the legal system as an accused or a party to a law suit, is a person without qualities, a "universal, abstract person." In Comack's view, however, this "Official Version of Law"[14] contains two fallacies.

First, while law seeks to be disinterested and just, and to exist outside of ideology, these commitments in themselves are a product of a very specific history and culture (2006: 22). In other words, far from having arrived at these ideas in a vacuum, invoking them points us back to historical experiences in western culture in which judges might have favoured family and friends, expressed bias toward enemies, or accepted benefits before rendering favourable judgments. Our concepts of justice and disinterest are rooted in this history, and it is a history that continues to evolve.

A second fallacy to the Official Version of Law that Naffine notes is that the abstract subject of law is not entirely without qualities (1990: 52). He or she is in fact always socially constructed by society at large and by agents in the legal system in particular. For example, the court, or the law itself, routinely takes into account a person's race, class, or gender — as in a youth sentencing hearing in which an offender is dealt with as an aboriginal female from a disadvantaged background. This practice imports the dangers of partial, rather than impartial, justice, since law's ideal subject is, in effect, always already endowed with certain qualities derived from our own social location, and our own prejudices and assumptions (Comack 2006: 22).

In *The Power to Criminalize*, Comack and Balfour advance the view that, far from being simply "a fair and impartial arbiter of social conflicts," the law must also be seen as "one of the sites in society that reproduces gender, race and class inequalities" (2004: 10). Legal actors do this acting within a world constituted by specific discourses of "masculinity, femininity, race, class and social space"; the law, as a result, is best understood not as "a set of rules and procedures, but a *process* that entails gendering, racializing and classing practices" (2004: 10).

Comack and Balfour set out in *The Power to Criminalize* an exemplary analysis of the processes by which certain discourses employed by legal actors perpetuate real inequalities in society. The ways in which anti-terror law reproduces inequalities for certain groups in particular, such as Arab and Muslim members of Canadian society, citizens and non-citizens alike, is a facet of my analysis but not the focus. I am interested, rather, in the way that Naffine, Comack, and Balfour's analyses shift the focus from specific legal developments or practices to their social context, and thereby "locate" law somewhere outside the text of the law itself. I am also interested in their challenge to the Official Version of Law as historical and cultural. We can infer from their approach that concepts central to the Official Version of Law, or the administration of justice, are never absolutely stable or closed.

In what follows, I explore how the law and practice of counter-terrorism deviates from the Official Version of Law by trying to renegotiate the conceptual framework that lies at the heart of our legal system. Counter-terror practices will also be seen to depart from the Official Version by virtue of the fact that in dealing with the figure of the suspected terrorist — a person who is neither a criminal nor an "enemy combatant," but something in between — we are dealing with a relationship between the law and its subject that raises yet another challenge to the notions of an objective and impartial tribunal, and a subject without qualities.

Concepts Central to the Administration of Justice

Before going further, I should explore briefly the concepts that I take to be central to the ideology or discourse that shapes the administration of justice. The notion of "due process" has roots that extend at least as far back as the English *Magna Carta* in the thirteenth century (Schwartz 1977: 2). The term refers to a host of procedural rights that have evolved from experiences with a range of injustices in English and American history. Some of these experiences included the exercise of excessive and arbitrary power by the sovereign or head of state; the use of arbitrary detention and lengthy delays in proceeding to trial; the use of secret evidence, or evidence obtained by torture; and the conduct of secret trials. By at least the early eighteenth century, however, a consensus had emerged in the Anglo-American tradition relating to what Ronald Dworkin has called "the vague but powerful idea of human dignity" (1977: 198). As Dworkin explains, this idea "associated with Kant, but defended by philosophers of different schools, supposes that there are ways of treating a man that are inconsistent with recognizing him (*sic*) as a full member of the human community, and holds that such treatment is profoundly unjust" (1977: 198). Jurists had come to appreciate the need to presume that a person accused of a crime is innocent until proven guilty in a fair trial that incorporates a certain "due process." This includes the right not to be arbitrarily detained; to be free from unreasonable search or seizure; to remain silent or to be protected from self-incrimination; to face one's accusers, or to know the case being made against oneself; and to be free from cruel and unusual punishment.

The constitutions of many western democracies, including those of Canada and the United States, have entrenched due-process rights among the nation's most basic and important laws. The *Canadian Charter of Rights* also makes specific reference to the primacy of the rule of law. This concept encapsulates much of the theory or ideology that purports to guide the administration of justice in Canada and elsewhere in the developed world. There is no single authoritative definition of its scope and meaning, but in 1885, the English legal scholar A.V. Dicey made a significant attempt in his *Introduction to the Study of the Law of the Constitution* (cited in Dicey 1965). He distinguished three meanings of the concept. First, it entails "the absolute supremacy or predominance of regular law as opposed to the influence of arbitrary power, and excludes the existence of arbitrariness, of prerogative, or even of wide discretionary authority on the part of the government" (1965: 202). Second, all are equal before the law and no one, regardless of his or her status, is exempt from the duty to obey the law. Third, the constitutional entrenchment of rights is "not the source but the consequence of rights."

Dicey's definition clearly suggests more than it states. W. Wesley Pue provides a more expansive definition, which sets out a number of propositions implied by Dicey's analysis:

1. All law should seek to attain minimal infringement of civil liberty.
2. There should be maximum clarity of definition regarding powers conferred, restrictions imposed, and offences created.
3. All exercise of governmental power should be accountable, visible, and reviewable by the ordinary courts in the ordinary ways. The *core* constitutional principle of responsible government requires clear and effective channels of political and legal accountability.
4. Secrecy should only be tolerated in the smallest possible zone,

only as absolutely essential, and only for limited duration. Power exercised in secret is never accountable.

5. Where extraordinary powers are invoked in times of perceived crisis, they should be of limited duration, renewable only by full reconsideration and re-enactment by Parliament. (2003: 270)

The "rule of law" is therefore something more than a synonym for constitutional supremacy. It implies the interrelated concepts of an independent and impartial judiciary, to ensure that all are subject to the law and are acting in accordance with the law. It also implies the notion of strict limits on the exercise of executive and police power, as well as strict adherence to the transparency of the exercise of that power, including holding anyone who exercises power on behalf of the state accountable. One question throughout this book will be how the law, policy, and practice of counter-terrorism departs from this conceptual apparatus, and whether this apparatus can accommodate the belief that those departures are sometimes necessary.

The Plan of the Book

In what follows, I explore the impact of counter-terrorism on the administration of justice in three contexts. The first chapter deals with Parliament's legislative response to September 11th. This involved a consensus between the governing Liberal Party, which held a majority of the seats in the House of Commons and Senate, and the official opposition, the "Conservative Alliance." (For this reason, I refer to Parliament instead of the government or the executive.) The second chapter looks at court cases that foreground the growing disparity between guiding principles in the law and legal solutions to problems in counter-terrorism. The third chapter explores the impact of the increasingly complex interrelations of law enforcement, intelligence, and other state agencies, and the expansion of state secrecy, on the principles of accountability and the rule of law.

In the first of the chapters that follow, I assess the options open to Parliament in the fall of 2001 when responding to what appeared to be a crisis or emergency. I argue that in passing the *Anti-Terrorism Act*, a majority of Parliamentarians created law that was clearly in violation of a number of constitutional rights, but that for reasons relating to the way that rights are limited in the Charter, and the way the limitation clause was likely to be interpreted in a climate of heightened fear, the Act could be described as "constitutional." This enabled the government to expand state powers in ways that might have been done by invoking emergency powers, or a temporary suspension of certain Charter rights. The government instead adopted a self-congratulatory rhetoric about having achieved a new balance between security and freedom, and a tidy consistency of anti-terror law with the constitution. This would help to establish a vocabulary of acquiescence that members of the judiciary, law enforcement, and review bodies would soon adopt. The key to this language is the belief that extraordinary measures, or a new approach to certain aspects of the administration of justice, are necessary to deal with the unprecedented challenges of terrorism itself.

In the next chapter, I focus on three problems with which the courts have dealt in the period after the *Anti-Terrorism Act* was passed: what to do with a suspected terrorist who faces the risk of torture if deported; whether to accept as constitutional the role of judges as interrogators in the aid of the state; and whether the security certificate regime is consistent with the rule of law. The court's response to each of these problems is marked by extreme differences of opinion and a number of inconsistent rulings: I explore these by looking in particular at interpretations of the Charter's guarantee of "life, liberty and security of the person" in section 7. These disparities point to a growing divide between conventional perspectives on the "principles of fundamental justice" and an evolving set of perspectives on these principles. The new perspectives can be gleaned from decisions that find "fundamental justice" consistent with the possibility of deportation where there is a risk of torture, or not inconsistent with the use of secret trials, secret intelligence, and the use of evidence obtained by torture. In each of these decisions, the view of "fundamental justice" is framed by a discourse of necessity and caution, or a new balance between freedom and the more elaborate demands of security.

The focus in the final chapter is the nexus of law enforcement and intelligence. With the inclusion of terrorism offences in the *Criminal Code* and amendments in the *Public Safety Act*, the national security mandate of the RCMP and other law enforcement agencies has become significantly broader. But the measures in place to ensure accountability — a crucial aspect of the rule of law — are inadequate to the challenges presented by the altered landscape. I explore ways in which the investigation and prosecution of suspected terrorists are bringing together a wider net of agencies and departments, with increased funding and more sophisticated tools. Both CSIS and the RCMP now work in close coordination with new entities, such as the Canadian Border Services Agency and the Financial Transactions and Reports Analysis Centre of Canada, and existing agencies, including the Coast Guard, the Canada Revenue Agency, Citizenship and Immigration Canada, and various municipal and provincial police forces. The RCMP is also assembling special "multi-agency law enforcement teams" that work with all levels of law enforcement in Canada and with their "international partners," exchanging information, resources and services.

The fact that so much cooperation and information sharing is taking place has many benefits: as the Air India Inquiry has affirmed, the lack of it can be disastrous. But the greater complexity and coordination among agencies poses a challenge to those who would seek to hold national security investigators accountable. An even greater set of challenges is posed by two further developments: the expansion of the scope of state secrecy in the *Canada Evidence Act*, and the dominance of a logic that can be traced from Parliament, through the courts, to the Arar Commission and beyond, in which an increase in secrecy and a lack of transparency are seen as necessary in all areas of national security, including the mechanisms for oversight and review. Where a high degree of confidentiality was once thought appropriate only for the review of civilian agencies such as CSIS and the Communications Security Establishment, it is now seen to be necessary for the police and other law enforcement entities as well. With more confidential hearings and secret reports likely in future inquiries and reviews of national security activities, public confidence in the accountability of law enforcement in the national security field will suffer more and more.

The concluding chapter summarizes the arguments of the book and questions the necessity for the *Anti-Terrorism Act* and other measures, including the wider scope of state secrecy. I argue that repealing the Act and relying on the law and policy in place before 2001 would help to bridge the gap between practice and principle in the administration of justice. The book then concludes with an exploration of avenues for bringing about change in counter-terror law and policy, including ways of raising public awareness of the issues and of promoting greater scepticism, among a range of stakeholders in the justice system, that extraordinary legal measures are prudent or necessary.

Notes

1. Adil Charkaoui, Hassan Almrei, Mohomed Harkat, Mahmoud Jaballah, and Mohammed Mahjoub.
2. For a summary of facts disclosed in Mohomed Mahjoub's case, see *Canada (Minister of Citizenship and Immigration) v. Mahjoub* (T.D.), 2001 FCT 1095, [2001] 4 F.C. 644.
3. Adil Charkaoui was identified by Ahmen Ressam and Abou Zubaida, although Ressam later recanted in a letter to Montreal journalist: <http://www.cbc.ca/canada/story/2007/08/22/charkaoui-court.html> (accessed on December 20, 2007).
4. *Re Jaballah*, 2006 FC 1230. This decision also includes a summary of the evidence disclosed in the case of Mahmoud Jaballah.
5. Justice Arthur Chaskalson, formerly of the Constitutional Court of South Africa, made this point as a member of the International Commission of Jurists' Eminent Jurists Panel on Terrorism, Counter-Terrorism and Human Rights in Toronto on April 24, 2007.
6. S.C. 2001, c. 27.

7. S.C. 2001, c. 41.
8. *R. v. Khawaja*, [2006] O.J. 4245.
9. R.S., 1985, c. C-5.
10. Section 38.
11. Section 38.
12. *Charkaoui v. Canada (Citizenship and Immigration)*, [2007] 1 S.C.R. 350, involved the appeals of Adil Charkaoui, Hassan Almrei, and Mohomed Harkat.
13. Bill C-3, 2nd Session, 39th Parliament, 2007.
14. This is Naffine's phrase (1990).

Chapter 1

Parliament, the *Anti-Terrorism Act,* and the Climate of Emergency

In the immediate aftermath of September 11th, 2001, lawmakers in Canada and many other nations were suddenly engrossed by the problem of terrorism. The United Nations Security Council passed Resolution 1373, which required all member nations to pass laws that would address terrorism, and especially the financing of terrorism, by the end of the year. Very soon, a majority of Parliamentarians in Ottawa had come to the consensus that the crisis called for significant changes to many areas of the law, going well beyond the requirements of Resolution 1373. The changes would relate primarily to the criminal law, but together they would have implications for the administration of justice in the broadest sense. To understand the nature and impact of these changes, I begin by assessing the climate of emergency in which they were made, and the options open to the government when it made them. I then look in more detail at key parts of the *Anti-Terrorism Act,* as well as commentary that assesses the Act in light of conventional legal principles. I conclude with a closer look at the part of the Act that amends the *Canada Evidence Act* to expand state privilege in ways that may have the most crucial impact on the administration of justice.

Parliament's actions in the fall of 2001 should first be understood in the context of the American and British responses to the same events. The executive in both the United Kingdom and the United States invoked a state of emergency soon after September 11th, and exercised a number of extraordinary powers.[1] President Bush issued a "military order" creating the power to declare a person an "unlawful combatant," to detain them indefinitely and to eventually try them before a military tribunal.[2] The Italian political theorist Giorgio Agamben noted:

> What is new about President Bush's order is that it radically erases any legal status of the individual, thus producing a legally unnamable and unclassifiable being. Not only do the Taliban captured in Afghanistan not enjoy the status of POWs as defined by the Geneva Convention, they do not even have the status of persons charged with a crime according to American laws. Neither prisoners nor persons accused, but simply "detainees," they are the object of a pure de facto rule, of a detention that is indefinite not only in the temporal sense but in its very nature as well, since it is entirely removed from the law and from judicial oversight. (2005: 3–4)

This is in part an overstatement, given that the U.S. Supreme Court has recognized that some of the detainees held at the American base in Guantánamo Bay, Cuba, possess certain rights.[3] However, Agamben's description captures the thrust what of Bush is attempting to do in Guantánamo. There has also been much discussion of the merit of Bush's strategy, and speculation as to whether he would suspend *habeas corpus*, as provided for in section 9, Article I of the U.S. Constitution: "when in Cases of Rebellion or Invasion the public Safety may require it."[4] In October of 2001, under the guise of normal lawmaking power, the U.S. Congress passed the *U.S.A. Patriot Act*,[5] which gave rise to a number of controversial powers that are beyond the scope of this study. But it is notable that even in the country that came directly under attack on September 11th, many of the anti-terror provisions crafted in response to the events were subject to a sunset clause. The Act itself was also clearly understood as a temporary, extraordinary measure that departed from any desirable standard of the constitutional freedoms that are central to American law and culture.

In London, the Labour government of Tony Blair had passed counter-terror legislation in 2000,[6] but following September 11th, it created many more invasive powers in a second round of legislation, titled the *Anti-Terrorism, Crime and Security Act, 2001*.[7] That Act followed the invocation of a state of emergency, as well as the issue of a "Derogation Order" by Britain's Home Secretary. Member states under the *European Convention on Human Rights* are required to issue such an order when seeking to make law in violation of its provisions. The order will only be valid, however, if the events that trigger the issuing of the order fall under the strict definition of an emergency set out in the *Convention*. Among the new powers that Britain asserted after issuing its derogation order were provisions in a second round of anti-terror legislation that allow for the indefinite detention of non-nationals who are not charged with a crime, and their deportation to nations where they might face torture.[8] In a 2004 appeal to the House of Lords, a group of detainees successfully challenged both the validity of the derogation order and the immigration detention provisions of the new Act.[9] Two further rounds of counter-terrorism legislation have followed in 2005 and 2006.[10] The first of these replaces indefinite detention of non-nationals with "control orders," which can entail a very restrictive form of house arrest and daily reporting to police. The second Act extends the amount of time that a terror suspect can be held without charge to twenty-eight days.

In Britain and America, therefore, there was a clear sense that power was being exercised in a temporary state of emergency, and that it would derogate from the normal scope of executive power. In Canada, by contrast, the government sought to exercise similar extraordinary powers, but without invoking or even explicitly acknowledging a state of emergency. This was possible in part because although Parliamentarians responded to September 11th in a spirit of heightened anxiety, bordering on a crisis or emergency, the precise extent of the danger remained unclear. As Irwin Cotler, a member of the governing Liberal Party of Canada, wrote in the fall of 2001:

> not a day has passed since Parliament convened on September 17 that has not been dominated by the cataclysmic events of September 11. Every party caucus, every meeting of the House Standing Committee on Justice and Human Rights, every Question Period, has been organized around the terrorist threat and the appropriate response. (2001: 111)

The events of September 11th were unpredictable and unprecedented, raising questions about further, more horrific acts of terrorism on American soil. It also seemed possible that Canada too had become a target, but this was cautious speculation at best.

The question for Parliamentarians, who were now inclined to support extraordinary measures, was whether to submit them to a time limit or make them permanent. The debate in Parliament was not over whether to invoke a state of emergency, in part because there was no clear cause to invoke one, but also (for reasons explored below) because Canadian law would arguably preclude this. Many politicians, journalists, and academics, however, took issue with the fact that controversial law was being made in a climate of emergency. An editorial in October of 2001 in one of Canada's national newspapers, *The Globe and Mail*, took the view that the anti-terrorism bill was a response to an emergency or crisis.[11] The editors called on the government to subject the entire bill to a sunset clause, because a crisis is "by definition finite." The very fact that a state of emergency had been invoked in the U.S and the U.K. added to the belief that any extraordinary measures invoked in the present climate should be temporary.

The government, however, forged ahead by tabling the *Anti-Terrorism Act* (Bill C-36), which would capitalize on the spirit of urgency and assert new and extraordinary powers for government, but make almost all of them permanent.[12] How the government rationalized this was a crucial part of its strategy: this rationalization would also help to shape attitudes towards the new anti-terror measures among other agents in the administration of justice. Given the controversial nature of the new law, a key issue for those following the debate in Parliament was whether the government understood the bill to amount to a temporary departure from the rule of law, or from basic Charter rights and values, and if so, whether and, in particular, why this was necessary.

The best indication of the government's intent in tabling Bill C-36 can be found in statements made in the House of Commons in October and November of 2001. Members of the Cabinet continued to insist — contrary to the views of most legal commentators — that the bill was consistent with the Constitution. The argument in support of this claim was never set out in any detail during the debate. But an assessment of the government's rhetoric in the context of how rights are limited in the Charter and how they were likely to be approached after September 11th in areas of national security, clearly reveals the implied logic of the government's position.

On first reading of Bill C-36 (October 15), then Minister of Justice, Anne McLellan, announced:

> Charter rights have been considered and preserved against the objectives of fighting terrorism and protecting national security. I assure everyone in the House and all Canadians that we have kept the individual rights and freedoms of Canadians directly in mind in developing these proposals.

Prime Minister Jean Chrétien was also confident that the bill was consistent with Canada's basic constitutional values. Speaking in the House later the same day, he stated:

> A free and open society never lightly increases the powers of law enforcement authorities. Our challenge in developing this legislation has been to respond in a way that reflects and protects, for the long term, our core values of freedom, democracy and equality....
>
> As the minister of justice, it was my privilege to introduce the Canadian Charter of Rights and Freedoms. I am deeply committed to it. I believe that the legislation we have introduced today is essential to preserving those very values. In the drafting of the anti-terrorism act, we have taken great care to protect these rights and freedoms. It provides meaningful protection of individual rights through the

inclusion of due process guarantees. It provides for a parliamentary review after three years to re-examine the necessity and effectiveness of these measures. I understand that today the minister said if it is needed earlier it will be earlier.

In the days following, however, there was no further mention by either the Prime Minister or the Minister of Justice of the need to subject the bill to an earlier review date — nor any movement on the issue when members of other parties urged that it be reduced to one year.[13] On second reading (October 16), McLellan's rhetoric became more inflated:

> Our world changed dramatically on September 11 but not in the manner that the terrorists who planned and carried out the horrific attacks had hoped. They aimed to frighten us, disrupt our lives and force us to question our most basic democratic values of freedom and liberty. They did not succeed. Our commitment to democracy is stronger than ever. Together all Canadians are committed to increasing public security while maintaining our core values.

By third reading (November 27th), her position was reduced to a series of blunt assertions. While members of the Conservative Alliance supported the bill, many other members raised concerns with various parts of it, and with the way it was being rushed through Parliament.

In spite of this, on third reading, McLellan urged members to forego further debate:

> Now is the time to move forward. Canadians expect their government to act to ensure their security and safety. Our allies around the world are moving and it would be irresponsible for us, as a government, not to move. A government's primary obligation is first and foremost to ensure the safety and security of its people.
>
> What we are doing in Bill C-36, and subsequently in Bill C-42, is putting in place the legal and operational infrastructure necessary to provide Canadians with that degree of safety and security that permits them to get on with their lives.[14]

By proposing to pass permanent legislation that would expand state power and curtail civil liberties, the government had come dangerously close, as David Dyzenhaus put it, to "stepping outside the rule of law" (2001: 27). In response to repeated calls to submit more, if not all, of the amendments to a sunset clause, McLellan stated:

> placing a sunset clause will impair efforts to identify and prosecute

terrorists and their supporters. A sunset clause for the entire bill would lead to a legislative vacuum. We cannot expect terrorism to disappear in a few years, thereby running the risk of not having effective laws in place for extended periods. (Cited by Dyzenhaus 2001: 27)

Against the objections of the New Democratic Party and the Bloc Quebecois, and criticism by many academics, jurists, and other interest groups, Bill C-36 was passed and brought into force on December 18, 2001.

A key moment in the critical assessment of the merits of Bill C-36 occurred at a conference at the University of Toronto in early November of that year, soon after the bill was first tabled. One of the issues at the conference was the question of making law in a time of emergency. A number of commentators took aim at many of McLellan's assertions. Kent Roach questioned whether it was necessary to create a new set of "terrorism" offences in the *Criminal Code*, or to fashion new tools to prevent terrorism. Expanding on this argument after the bill was passed, Ziyaad Mia suggested that arguments for the necessity of new measures

> ignore the array of provisions in the *Criminal Code* which may be used effectively to prevent terrorist acts before they are committed. For example, Part XIII of the *Criminal Code* [which is headed: "Attempts — Conspiracies — Accessories"] criminalizes a wide range of activities, both inside and outside of Canada, where two or more people conspire to commit an offence. In other words, criminal activity can be prevented before it takes place. Since terrorist acts are already subject to the *Criminal Code*, it follows that Part XIII may be used to prevent terrorist acts that are on the drawing board. (2003: 128)

David Dyzenhaus and others took aim at McLellan's assertion that a sunset clause would leave a "legal vacuum" if invoked. Dyzenhaus countered:

> the *point* of the Bill is to *create* a legal vacuum. The Bill is designed to remove, in so far as the Charter permits this, law-enforcement and intelligence gathering activities from the discipline of the rule of law. And by rule of law here I mean simply the general principles of the common law of judicial review that require openness and accountability of officials when they make decisions affecting important individual interests. (2001: 27)

For Dyzenhaus, all anti-terror statutes depart from the rule of law to the extent that they grant the government at its discretion the power to define who is a terrorist — and effectively shield that decision from the scrutiny of the courts. "It will be for the agents of law-enforcement and security to tell us who the terrorist is, when they have him in their grasp" (2001: 27). This, combined with the intent to make an indefinite change in the law, amounted to a marked departure from the rule of law. Dyzenhaus notes that: "even if sunset clauses are introduced, the fact that what we have is not emergency legislation but a terrorism law — an emergency law masquerading as an ordinary statute — means that we have stepped outside the rule of law" (2001: 28).

How, then, could the government persist in the view that such legislation was necessary, and also consistent with both Charter rights and values — including the rule of law?

What Might Have Been
(Parliament's Options after September 11th)

The options open to the government at this juncture are essential to understanding its strategy. Lorraine Weinrib, a contributor to the October conference, attempted to assess these options in some detail (2001: 93–108). She was particularly critical of the government's decision not to frame its response to September 11th as a temporary, emergency measure. She arrived at a similar conclusion to that of Dyzenhaus by arguing that the government's decision not to invoke Canada's statutory machinery of emergency derogation amounts to an exercise of power reminiscent of that under the now repealed *War Measures Act* (1914).

Weinrib considered two alternative courses that Parliament might have taken. First, rights might have been temporarily suspended by recourse to the "notwithstanding" clause of the Charter (section 33). This clause allows either federal or provincial governments to suspend the operation of certain rights in the Charter (including all of the "legal rights") for a period of five years, with the possibility of renewing the suspension. This would seem to allow for a derogation of rights in a time of emergency; but Weinrib suggests two reasons why this reading of the Charter would be contrary to the intent of its authors — contrary, that is, to the hope that the Charter would make it more difficult to derogate from civil rights in an emergency situation.

First, Weinrib argues that if the framers had intended section 33 to function as an emergency derogation clause, they would have included language to that effect (2001: 98). She notes that in a number of western nations that have created constitutional instruments after the Second World War, entrenched derogation clauses have included a detailed set of conditions for the suspension of rights.[15] This is conspicuously absent in section 33 of the Charter. By opting not to follow the approach taken by drafters of post-war bills of rights, Canadians were making clear that "their complaint against the Charter was its restraint on political power generally, not specifically in times of emergency" (2001: 98). As Weinrib points out, the models for section 33 were the provisions in federal and provincial statutes that allow for the suspension of other provisions — and these were rarely, if ever, invoked. The implication was that invoking section 33 would seem excessive, given the fact that it is not set out in the Charter as an emergency derogation clause. The relatively rare use of the notwithstanding clause in the Charter's history, prior to September 11th, would also have added to the appearance of immoderation if it had been invoked after September 11.

A second option open to Parliament at that time was to pass counter-terrorism legislation pursuant to an invocation of a state of emergency under the relatively new *Emergencies Act* (1988). This Act was a reworking of the *War Measures Act*, which served as Canada's governing law on emergency power from 1914 to 1988. Weinrib had drawn upon the work of Patricia Peppin to underscore the point that prior to the Charter, the *War Measures Act* had been invoked on a number of occasions to allow for various injustices on the part of the Canadian government. As Peppin writes,

> Citizenship, the right to hold property, freedom to contract, the right to bring a civil suit, freedom of speech, freedom of the press, freedom of association, *habeas corpus*, equality before the law, due process, the right to a fair trial, the presumption of innocence and the rule of law itself have all been denied in greater and lesser measure under the *War Measures Act*. (Peppin 1993: 131, cited by Weinrib 2001: 100)

The Act allowed for an inordinate degree of concentrated, unchecked power in the executive. Its most memorable use in recent years was in response to the "October crisis" of 1970, which involved terrorist acts on the part of the *Front de libération du Québec*. Invoking powers under the Act, the Liberal government of Pierre Trudeau ordered the arrest and detention without charge of hundreds of civilians, thus leaving a lasting impression of the Act as the enabling instrument for an excessive display of executive power in a time of peace.

Parliament sought to remedy the issue by entrenching a bill of rights in the Constitution in 1982, but also by revoking the *War Measures Act* and replacing it with the *Emergencies Act* in 1988.[16] The new Act provides a much more stringent framework for the invocation of emergency powers by limiting the assertion of those powers to a specific duration, and by dispersing the power to invoke or continue a state of emergency among a wider group of Parliamentarians (as opposed to the executive alone). Weinrib highlighted, among other features of the Act, that both houses of Parliament must confirm the invocation of a state of emergency, and the fact that any law made during the period of emergency must be considered by Parliament as a whole within two sitting days (2001: 102). She also noted that

> the Act authorizes the Cabinet [to] make orders and regulations under the authority of the proclamation of emergency. These powers are extensive and as invasive of existing rights and liberties as the provisions made a permanent component of Canadian law under Bill 36. The powers are however temporary. They are also subject to the ongoing involvement of Parliament.

Weinrib's broader point was that the Liberal government had chosen not to invoke the *Emergencies Act* at this juncture at least in part because it believed Bill C-36 would survive Charter scrutiny under section 1. As McLellan had put it in the House of Commons, "the balance between individual and collective security shifted after the attacks" (cited by Weinrib 2001: 97). The implication for Weinrib was that invoking the *Emergencies Act* was therefore unnecessary, and avoiding it would afford the government greater leeway.

But if the government had pursued Weinrib's second option, it remains unclear whether it would in fact have been lawful to declare a state of emergency in these circumstances. Would the nature of the threat posed by September 11th pass the new test for an emergency? Weinrib conjectured that of the four possible emergency scenarios proposed by the Act, Bill C-36 might have been preceded by a proclamation under the heading, "international emergency" (2001: 97). Section 27 of the Act defines this as:

> an emergency involving Canada and one or more other countries that arises from acts of intimidation or coercion or the real or imminent use of serious force or violence and that is so serious as to be a national emergency.

Conceivably, the "involvement" of one or more nations here need not be in an adversarial capacity. If there was some connection to Canada in the events of September 11th, this might have made sense. Without one, this ground of emergency might not have withstood a challenge.[17]

Among the three other classes of emergency in the Act, two clearly would not apply. A "public welfare emergency" (section 5), involves a natural disaster, an outbreak of disease, or an accident or pollution; and a "war emergency" (section 37), refers "war or other armed conflict, real or imminent, involving Canada or any of its allies that is so serious as to be a national emergency." The fourth class of emergency, however, might have been applicable: a "public order emergency" (section 16), which is defined as "an emergency that arises from threats to the security of Canada and that is so serious as to be a national emergency." "Threats to the security of Canada" has the meaning assigned by section 2 of the *Canadian Security Intelligence Service Act*, which states that it may include:

(*a*) espionage or sabotage that is against Canada or is detrimental to the interests of Canada or activities directed toward or in support of such espionage or sabotage,

(*b*) foreign influenced activities within or relating to Canada that are detrimental to the interests of Canada and are clandestine or deceptive or involve a threat to any person,

(*c*) activities within or relating to Canada directed toward or in support of the threat or use of acts of serious violence against persons or property for the purpose of achieving a political, religious or ideological objective within Canada or a foreign state, and

(*d*) activities directed toward undermining by covert unlawful acts, or directed toward or intended ultimately to lead to the destruction or overthrow by violence of, the constitutionally established system of government in Canada,

but does not include lawful advocacy, protest or dissent, unless carried on in conjunction with any of the activities referred to in paragraphs (*a*) to (*d*).

In each of these cases, the activity in question requires a connection to Canada. Whether there was one on September 11th is arguable at best.

For these reasons, a declaration of emergency under Canadian law in the wake of September 11th may not have been legally viable. In any case, perhaps the primary reason the governing Liberals declined to pursue this option (Bill C-36) is that it would have seemed heavy-handed and excessive to invoke a state of emergency in Canada at that time. Comparisons with the use of emergency powers in the "October crisis" would have been unavoidable. Similarly, the government would likely have faced severe criticism if it had invoked the "notwithstanding" clause. The path of least resistance was also one that allowed the government to table its bill with a great display of commitment to the values of the Constitution. This middle course was made possible, to a large extent, by the structure of the Charter itself, and in particular by the inclusion and precise wording of the Charter's limitation clause.

The rights set out in the Charter are limited by its opening section, which allows for lawful violations of rights where these can be "demonstrably justified." Weinrib had pointed out the irony of the fact that the drafters of section 1 had sought to narrow the range of circumstances in which rights could be justifiably limited; however, the example they had in mind happened to be none other than a terrorist crisis on Canadian soil (2001: 97). Since

Trudeau's invocation of the *War Measures Act* in 1970 was still well within the memory of the general public, it served to emphasize the need for the constitutional entrenchment of individual rights and the strict circumscription of emergency powers. An earlier proposal for section 1 would have allowed "reasonable limits as are generally accepted in a free and democratic society with a parliamentary system of government" (cited by Weinrib 2001: 97). But as Weinrib writes,

> Of particular importance was the generally held view that past breaches of fundamental freedoms in Canada under the *War Measures Act* would pass muster under this [proposed] standard. One of the primary legal purposes of the Charter was to ensure that emergency conditions no longer authorize unjustifiable encroachments on these fundamental freedoms. (2001: 97)

The final formulation reads: "The *Canadian Charter of Rights and Freedoms* guarantees the rights and freedoms set out in it subject only to such reasonable limits prescribed by law as can be demonstrably justified in a free and democratic society."

The omission of the words "emergency" and "crisis" in the Charter suggest, however, that the drafters still thought it possible that emergency conditions could justify a limiting of rights, but that the government should be pressed to prove why this would be reasonable and necessary. Among all of the options open to the government in the fall of 2001, this clearly seemed the most prudent, but not only because, as Weinrib had suggested, it would give the government the most leeway. The government's rhetoric also makes clear that the powers of the *Anti-Terrorism Act* were justified in their indefinite form precisely because after September 11th, measures that might once have seemed extraordinary were now reasonable and necessary for effective national security. From this new perspective, the measures in the Act were neither excessive nor extraordinary; they were a reasonable response to what had become the new normal.

We are left, then, with the record of two debates from that period and shortly afterwards. In the one that took place on Parliament Hill, a majority saw the need for a number of significant amendments to the law that would alter the practical workings of the administration of justice in Canada in fundamental ways. In the debate among legal commentators, the media, jurists, and various interest groups, the proposed legislation bore the markings of a growing divide between the practical workings of our justice system and the theory and principles meant to guide it.[18] In what follows, I explore some of the latter debate with a view to highlighting the divide in question.

The Definition of Terrorism (A Closer Look at the Act)

Section 83.01 of the *Criminal Code* defines "terrorist activity" as, among other things, an act committed "for a political, religious or ideological purpose, objective or cause."[19] A number of commentators criticized this feature of the definition on the basis that, as Irwin Cotler put it, "a motivational requirement... stands in stark contrast to the criminal law's historical refusal to either require motive for conviction or excuse conduct by reason of lack of motive" (2003: 35). Others noted that a group might be deemed "terrorist" for following an ideology contrary to that of the prosecution or the government. See also Don Stuart (2001: 208), and David Schneiderman and Brenda Cossman (2001: 183). Ziyaad Mia, of the Muslim Lawyers' Association of Toronto, wrote that "the inherent problem in defining 'terrorist activity,' and hence, 'terrorism' is that one man's terrorism is another man's liberation struggle" (2003: 130). Mia feared that the definition of terrorism in the Act could be used as a tool for political suppression, especially in cases relating to groups acting outside of Canada. He argued:

> History has borne out that effective civil disobedience, political and social activism sometimes require forms of advocacy that may involve violence, for example in the form of armed resistance to attack, occupation or oppression.... The exception to "terrorist activity" carved out in the [*Anti-Terrorism Act*] would have offered no protection to Nelson Mandela and the African National Congress, or fighters in the French Resistance to Nazi occupation. (2003: 131)

Mia also questioned whether the definition of "terrorist activity" would apply to a group that resisted, by acts of violence, the regimes of Saddam Hussein or Robert Mugabe. By taking sides, as it were, and applying the definition to one group and not another, the law would be "delegitimiz[ed]... by injecting subjective political concerns" (2003: 131).

Kent Roach has pointed to two further consequences of including motive in the definition of terrorism. A failure to prove motive can lead to an acquittal of a terrorist charged for some nefarious act of significant magnitude (2003: 26). The question would then be raised whether the person could be accused of committing the act itself (for instance, murder) if motive was not established beyond a reasonable doubt. Section 662 of the *Criminal Code* allows for findings of guilt of lesser included offences, but the question might arise in a prosecution on a charge of "terrorist activity" as to precisely which other offences this charge would contain (as "lesser included" offences).

Roach has also noted that by criminalizing motive on religious, political or ideological grounds, the prosecution of terrorism offences necessarily becomes a trial about religious, political, and ideological issues — as opposed to a trial on whether the act was committed (2003: 27). Police would be required in this context to gather information about and investigate a suspect's beliefs and religious practices — a task for which the police are not well equipped. Suspects in this context would all too easily run the risk of blurring "the line between terrorism and radical political or religious dissent" (Roach 2003: 27).

The Element of Intent

In addition to defining a "terrorist activity," the Act includes a definition of a "terrorism offence" and a number of provisions that, together, have the effect of reclassifying certain actions as "terrorism offences," including highjacking an airplane or financing a terrorist group.[20] It also includes the act of "facilitating" or "participating in" terrorism, or a "terrorist organization."

A number of commentators had questioned whether the offence of "facilitating" contains a sufficient *mens rea* component (i.e., whether it is necessary to prove the element of intent). The provision (section 83.19 of the *Criminal Code*) states:

> (1) Every one who knowingly facilitates a terrorist activity is guilty of an indictable offence and liable to imprisonment for a term not exceeding fourteen years.
> (2) For the purposes of this Part, a terrorist activity is facilitated whether or not
> (a) the facilitator knows that a particular terrorist activity is facilitated;
> (b) any particular terrorist activity was foreseen or planned at the time it was facilitated; or
> (c) any terrorist activity was actually carried out.

For Roach, "this wording goes beyond watering down the fault element to obliterating it" (2003: 35). The key is subsection 2(b). If the accused is not aware that an activity is foreseen or planned, how can he or she "knowingly" facilitate? Roach conjectured that the only remaining fault element here would be "failing to take reasonable care to ensure that what was being facilitated was actually not a terrorist activity." A person could therefore be convicted of facilitating terrorism without knowing they were in fact facilitating terrorism.

Participating in Terrorism

The wording of the participation offence is worth citing in some detail to appreciate how broadly it could be interpreted and how minimal a role the element of intent plays here as well:

> (1) Every one who knowingly participates in or contributes to, directly or indirectly, any activity of a terrorist group for the purpose of enhancing the ability of any terrorist group to facilitate or carry out a terrorist activity is guilty of an indictable offence and liable to imprisonment for a term not exceeding ten years. ...
> (3) Participating in or contributing to an activity of a terrorist group includes
> (*a*) providing, receiving or recruiting a person to receive training;
> (*b*) providing or offering to provide a skill or an expertise for the benefit of, at the direction of or in association with a terrorist group;
> (*c*) recruiting a person in order to facilitate or commit
> (i) a terrorism offence, or
> (ii) an act or omission outside Canada that, if committed in Canada, would be a terrorism offence;
> (*d*) entering or remaining in any country for the benefit of, at the direction of or in association with a terrorist group;

A number of bar associations across Canada were concerned that 3(b) would capture the act of providing legal representation to persons accused of terrorism; however, the concern was ignored (Stuart 2003: 157). Many argued that the scenarios set out in subsection (3) would likely be found unconstitutional for being vague or overbroad (Stuart 2003: 157). Kent Roach noted that the offence in 2(b) "may be committed whether or not the accused's participation or contribution actually enhances the ability of a terrorist group to carry out a terrorist activity" (2003: 43).

An Early Test of the Provisions

The aspects of the *Anti-Terrorism Act* discussed thus far were challenged in the first prosecution under the Act, an Ontario case called *R. v. Khawaja*[21] (currently in progress). It is worth addressing this decision briefly to appreciate how the court has interpreted the provisions, and how a court might interpret other aspects of the Act.

The accused in this case is charged with a number of the new terrorism offences in the *Criminal Code*, including participating and facilitating.[22] The challenge was heard in December of 2005, before Justice Rutherford of the

Ontario Superior Court of Justice, and related primarily to the definition of terrorism (section 83.01) and the *mens rea* element in a number of the provisions reviewed above. The challenge was made in a preliminary motion (before evidence had been called in the case), and was worded in this way:

> The Applicant brings this Application seeking a declaration that sections 83.01(1), 83.03(a), 83.18, 83.18(1), 83.18(3)(a), 83.19, 83.2, and 83.21(1) are of no force and effect pursuant to section 52(1) of the *Constitution Act, 1982*, on the basis that the provisions are vague and/or over-broad, they dilute the essential fault requirements of criminal law, and they infringe his rights to freedom of association, freedom of conscience and religion, and freedom of thought, belief, opinion, and expression pursuant to section 2 of the Charter.[23]

The court declined to find any of the provisions void for vagueness or over-broad in their reach. They were not vague because "they describe conduct in a fashion that provides notice of what is prohibited and set an intelligible standard for both citizen and law enforcement officials."[24] The impugned provisions were not overbroad because they had "sufficiently clear meanings."[25]

On the question of whether the *mens rea* in some of the provisions (conspiracy, providing assistance) was diluted to the point of being non-existent, as some had argued, the court took the opposite view:

> Returning then to the qualifying provisions that it is suggested may water down or even obliterate the required *mens rea*, it seems to me that they do not do more than allow for the subjective guilty knowledge to be non-specific, lacking in detail or generalized. They also allow for culpability when the object of a guilty intent goes unrealized, or is wasted. It is unnecessary that an accused be shown to have knowledge of the specific nature of terrorist activity he intends to aid, support, enhance or facilitate, as long as he knows it is terrorist activity in a general way. It doesn't have to be shown that an accused actually facilitated terrorist activity as long as it can be shown that he intended to do so. It doesn't matter if an accused knows the identity of the one he instructs to carry out terrorist activity, as long as he knowingly instructs someone to do so. And so on.
>
> These so called erosions or diluents do not, in my view, significantly reduce the moral opprobrium or fault requirement of the accusations open under sections 83.18, .19 and .21 merely because of the lack of details or specifics of the operation. While the specific qualifying provisions spelled out in these sections would seem to be a response to the type of cellularized activity the Parliamentary

Committees were warned of in the evidence of such witnesses as Mr. Kennedy and Mr. Mosley, the provisions also reflect common law principles that have long been part of our criminal conspiracy law.[26]

The court did, however, find that the inclusion of a "political, religious or ideological purpose" in the definition of "terrorist activity" (section 83.01(1)(b)(i)(A)) was contrary to the freedoms protected in section 2 of the Charter:

It seems to me that the inevitable impact to flow from the [motive] requirement in the definition of "terrorist activity" will be to focus investigative and prosecutorial scrutiny on the political, religious and ideological beliefs, opinions and expressions of persons and groups both in Canada and abroad. Equally inevitable will be the chilling effect Webb predicts. There will also be an indirect or re-bound effect of the sort Professor Stribopoulos described, as individuals' and authorities' attitudes and conduct reflect the shadow of suspicion and anger falling over all who appear belong to or have any connection with the religious, political or ideological grouping identified with specific terrorist acts. This in my view amounts to a *prima facie* infringement.[27]

The infringement could not be justified on a section 1 analysis, because it did not "minimally impair" the rights in question.[28] As Rutherford J. put it, "the provision used to narrow the focus leads inevitably to putting the searchlights of investigative and enforcement activity, and the attention of the public, on some of the freedom-protected aspects of the lives of those on whom any shadow of suspicion may fall, with or without justification."[29]

As it stands, without the motive element in the definition of "terrorist activity," the Crown now has less to prove in its case against the accused than it did at the outset.

Preventive Detention

These provisions are one of two aspects of the *Anti-Terrorism Act*, which were subject to a five-year sunset clause and which lapsed in 2007. (A bill currently before the Senate, however, proposes to restore them.)[30] It should suffice here to say that, to many commentators, the detention provisions constituted "novel *demarch* in criminal investigations and procedure" (Cotler 2003: 43). They allow for a person's arrest and detention *before* a crime has taken place — where there are reasonable grounds to suspect a terrorist activity "will be carried out" or that the arrest is necessary to "prevent the carrying out of the terrorist activity."[31] Cotler argued that the provisions contain a number of "due process" protections, including the requirement that any perceived threat be specific and involve the person in particular; that, except in "exigent circumstances," the Attorney General's consent be given before making an arrest; and the provision for judicial review of the detention. But Cotler also noted that "the Act would allow warrantless arrest and detention on a mere suspicion that a terrorist activity is planned, without the need for a reasonable belief that the activity is in any way imminent" (2003: 43).

Mia was more critical of the provisions on the grounds of due process. He argued that they mark a "drastic departure from Charter and criminal law standards" and that, in particular, they violate four "legal" protections in the Charter: protection from arbitrary detention, the right to be informed promptly of the reasons for arrest or detention, the right to be informed of the *specific* offence, and the right to have the detention reviewed by way of *habeas corpus* (2003: 134). Mia also questioned the need for the provisions by noting that section 495 of the *Criminal Code* enables an officer to arrest without warrant "a person who has committed an indictable offence or who, on reasonable grounds, he believes has committed or is about to commit an indictable offence" (2003: 128). This was a sufficient tool for preventative action on the part of law enforcement. By contrast, the new provisions allow for arrest and detention on a mere hunch, without the officer providing for a prompt explanation of the grounds of arrest, and it allowed for a delay in bail or review.

Investigative Hearings

The second set of provisions now lapsed pursuant to the sunset clause were those dealing with investigative hearings. (The current Senate bill proposes to restore these as well.) They would enable a judge to compel a person to appear before the court to answer questions posed by the Crown; to charge a person with contempt for refusing to answer; and to issue an arrest warrant for those who fail or refuse to appear.[32] The provisions also give courts the broad power to impose on the hearing any "terms or conditions that the judge considers desirable, including terms... for the protection of any ongoing investigation."[33] This has been interpreted to allow for the conduct of these hearings *in camera*.[34] Cotler contended that the Act included a number of safeguards over the exercise of this power, including the requirement for reasonable grounds to believe a terrorist offence has been or will be committed; protection from self-incrimination; and powers to protect the interests of witnesses compelled to testify (2003: 44). Cotler also noted the power to force a person to testify is not new in Canadian law. Persons can be compelled to testify in coroners' inquiries and public inquiries, and also in criminal proceedings, pursuant to section 545 of the *Criminal Code*. That section of the *Code* provides for persons to be compelled to testify in a preliminary inquiry, which is a hearing held in a case where charges are laid in an indictable matter and the purpose of the hearing is to determine whether there is sufficient merit to the accusations to proceed to a full trial. But Cotler shared the concern of the Canadian Bar Association that investigative hearings bring the criminal law closer to an "inquisitorial model" by curtailing the right to silence — despite the inclusion in the provision of a protection from self-incrimination.

While Cotler was correct to point out that the notion of forcing a person to give evidence is not new, the prominence of the concept itself of investigative hearings in the broader framework of anti-terror prosecutions, as contemplated by Bill C-36, arguably was new. The inclusion of a provision dedicated to this subject in a new chapter of the *Criminal Code* dealing with terrorism demonstrates a significant shift towards an inquisitorial approach to evidence in terrorism cases.

The investigative hearing provisions were invoked in a proceeding linked to the "Air India" trial,[35] and resulted in a constitutional challenge before the Supreme Court of Canada.[36] The majority upheld the provision as constitutional (for reasons I explore in the next chapter). But in the dissenting opinion of Justices LeBel and Fish, the provision compromised "the institutional dimension of judicial independence" and should be declared unconstitutional. A judge presiding over an investigative hearing might be impartial, they reasoned, but the process would turn the courts into a branch of the executive. The judge's role in such a hearing would be reduced to little more than acting as a tool to facilitate a Crown or police investigation. Also, the justices found that the section does not equip the judge with the means to "effectively play his or her role as protector of the fundamental rights of the person being examined."[37] Furthermore, investigations held *in camera* would add to the perception that the judiciary and the executive in these hearings were not acting independently of one another. They noted as well that "the judge's duties under s. 83.38 are unlike any of the duties traditionally discharged by the judiciary."

In addition to these arguments, one key difference that makes investigative hearings exceptional and unusual in the criminal law is the fact that although witnesses can be compelled to testify in trials, or preliminary hearings, they cannot be compelled to testify in the investigative stages of a case. The investigative hearings are exceptional because they can be invoked before anyone has been charged with an offence. They are an extraordinary tool available to the Crown to carry out an investigation that breaches the privacy rights of persons not clearly involved in an offence. Martha Shaffer has noted that until Bill C-36, there was "no requirement under Canadian law that ordinary citizens assist police officers in their investigations, and certainly no power that would permit a person to effectively be detained, compelled to attend a hearing, and to answer questions for this purpose" (2001: 197). Other commentators have pointed out that these provisions mark a departure from "the rule in our criminal law system that there can be no trials *in absentia*, that is, in the absence of the accused, so that he may be present to protect his rights in the criminal process" (CAUT 2005: 35).

Wiretapping

The *Anti-Terrorism Act* also enables the Minister of National Defence to authorize the "Communications Security Establishment" to intercept communications between persons outside Canada and those inside Canada.[38] The power to authorize wiretapping here is restricted to "the sole purpose of obtaining foreign intelligence" and the "sole purpose of protecting the computer systems or networks of the Government of Canada."[39] But as the authors of a later Parliamentary submission on the Act have noted, "there is no express prohibition on the [Communications Security Establishment] giving information to law enforcement about Canadians" (CAUT 2005: 40). Moreover, Cotler, among others, has taken issue with the fact that a minister can issue a warrant for wiretapping without first obtaining a court's approval. He pointed out that if authorization is not subject to judicial confirmation, the "security establishment" could be eavesdropping on any number of communications without any public or independent oversight whatsoever (Colter 2003: 42).

A List of Terrorist Entities

Section 83.05 of the bill sets out a scheme by which the Solicitor General of Canada can recommend to the Governor in Council that groups be added to a list of "entities" deemed to be "terrorist groups."[40] Once added to the list, a group's property may be seized, and persons involved with the group can be charged if their involvement "enhances the ability" of the group to carry out a terrorist activity.[41] Cotler noted the low standard the government is required to meet here (2003: 46). The Solicitor General can allege a belief that an entity "has knowingly carried out, attempted to carry out, participated in or facilitated a terrorist activity," with only "reasonable grounds" for the belief. And she or he is not required to present evidence in support of the belief.[42]

Cotler also noted that, although the decision to add a group to the list can be challenged by way of judicial review, this safeguard operates "after the fact" (2003: 43). It would be preferable to give notice to an entity and allow for a response before making the decision than to make it first and review it later. For Stuart, allowing for review only after being added to the list violates the presumption of innocence guaranteed in section 11(d) of the

Charter (2003: 156). The Act also includes various obstacles for any entity seeking review of the decision to list it as a terrorist entity. Section 83.05(6) mandates that the judge to do the following:

> (a) examine, in private, any security or criminal intelligence reports considered in listing the applicant and hear any other evidence or information that may be presented by or on behalf of the Solicitor General and may, at the request of the Solicitor General, hear all or part of that evidence or information in the absence of the applicant and any counsel representing the applicant, if the judge is of the opinion that the disclosure of the information would injure national security or endanger the safety of any person;
>
> (b) provide the applicant with a statement summarizing the information available to the judge so as to enable the applicant to be reasonably informed of the reasons for the decision, without disclosing any information the disclosure of which would, in the judge's opinion, injure national security or endanger the safety of any person;
>
> (c) provide the applicant with a reasonable opportunity to be heard; and
>
> (d) determine whether the decision is reasonable on the basis of the information available to the judge and, if found not to be reasonable, order that the applicant no longer be a listed entity.

The notion of the court examining evidence to decide whether it should be disclosed to the accused (or, in this case, the party alleged to be culpable) is not new. The provisions in sections 278.2 to 9 of the *Criminal Code* provide for the examination, by the court, of medical and psychiatric records of complainants in sexual assault cases — before they can be disclosed to the accused. However, there are a number of important differences between the two contexts — these differences are indicative of a deeper shift in the approach to balancing the rights of the accused and the state.

In the earlier framework for disclosure, section 278.2(3) states that "in the case of *a* record in respect of which this section applies that is in the possession or control of the prosecutor, the prosecutor shall notify the accused that the record is in the prosecutor's possession" [emphasis added]. In this case, the state has an obligation to disclose the existence of any record of which the Crown has knowledge. In section 83.05(6), the state (or the Solicitor General) is not under the same duty to disclose all relevant information. Arguably, the wording in section 83.05(6)(a) is permissive of a more selective disclosure to the court of the evidence relied upon by the state in forming its belief.

A second key difference in the two contexts is that, in the sexual assault provisions, the court can order the production of a record from a third party.[43] Under section 83.05(6), the judge cannot order a third party — such as CSIS or any of the agencies assisting the Solicitor General — to disclose a record to the court or the accused entity. So, for example, if the accused entity has knowledge of a document on which the Solicitor General is relying, and the document has not been disclosed to the court, there would be no way of compelling disclosure of that document to either the court or the accused.

A third key difference is the grounds for disclosure. Sections 278.7(1) to (6) require the judge to balance the complainant's (or record-holder's) privacy interests with the accused's right to make full answer and defence.[44] In section 83.05(6)(a) and (b), there is to be no disclosure to the applicant, and the applicant's counsel can even be excluded from the hearing of the evidence, if the judge deems this necessary in the interest of "national security." In other words, the section contemplates not a balancing but an almost complete compromise of the applicant's rights in favour of the state's interest.

One key flaw in the newer scheme is that it assumes that a judge is qualified to assess whether the disclosure of certain information would "injure national security" or endanger a person's safety. There is no test in the Act to assist the court in making this determination. Furthermore, section 83.05(6)(b) asks the court to do something which could be considered extraordinary in the criminal law: to "provide the applicant with a statement summarizing the information available" without disclosing that which would be injurious or unsafe. In the scheme under section 278, the judge's ultimate role is to order disclosure, not summarize it.

Another unusual feature of the list scheme is the scope of evidence that may form a part of the review. Section 83.05(6.1) states:

> The judge may receive into evidence anything that, in the opinion of the judge, is reliable and appropriate, even if it would not otherwise be admissible under Canadian law, and may base his or her decision on that evidence.

A further provision, 85.06, allows for an even broader scope:

> (1) For the purposes of subsection 83.05(6), in private and in the absence of the applicant or any counsel representing it,
> (a) the Solicitor General of Canada may make an application to the judge for the admission of information obtained in confidence from a government, an institution or an agency of a foreign state, from an international organization of states or from an institution or an agency of an international organization of states; and
> (b) the judge shall examine the information and provide counsel

representing the Solicitor General with a reasonable opportunity to be heard as to whether the information is relevant but should not be disclosed to the applicant or any counsel representing it because the disclosure would injure national security or endanger the safety of any person.

These provisions raise the possibility of an entity being declared a "terrorist group" based on information obtained from a foreign state that used torture in the process of obtaining the information, or a state that had closer ties to Canada than to the group in question. The information in turn could be used to prosecute a person in Canada with alleged ties to the listed entity. The Evangelical Fellowship of Canada, which made submissions to Parliament in the fall of 2001, provided another example (Pue 2003: 46). The Fellowship's concern was that some of the humanitarian and charity work it does abroad might run contrary to the interests of certain foreign governments or entities. "False or misleading" information provided to Canada could result in its becoming a listed entity, or the fear of this possibility could result in a "chilling effect" on the part of international charitable organizations in Canada.

To recap, then, the party calling for judicial review in this context would be precluded from receiving full disclosure of the evidence upon which the decision was made, and even the court could be precluded from reviewing all of the available relevant evidence. This could occur if the Solicitor General, or CSIS, provided only selective disclosure of available evidence to the court (either out of a fear that full disclosure would compromise national security, or because the investigative agency, or the Solicitor General, took a different view of what evidence was "relevant" to the hearing). These issues arise at least in part because the provision dispenses with the presumption of innocence. It also allows for what amounts to a finding of guilt before a fair trial, and the review provision contemplates a challenge without the benefit of full answer and defence.

Expanding Privilege and the Scope of State Secrecy

In recent years, Canada's Parliament has passed a number of bills dealing with access to information and the protection of state secrets. The amendments to the *Canada Evidence Act*[45] in Bill C-36 are among the most significant. They expand considerably the scope of the assertion of what is called "public interest immunity"; they bring about unprecedented obligations on all members of the public to protect sensitive information; and they curtail the right to appeal the state's assertion of privilege. The scope of state secrecy is now so broad that it marks what might be the most serious departure in Bill C-36 from basic principles of the administration of justice.[46]

Bill C-36 replaced both the statutory scheme for the state's assertion of "public interest immunity" and the assertion of privilege over certain information (Stewart 2001: 217). Before the bill was enacted, sections 37 to 39 of the *Canada Evidence Act* allowed for a process by which the Crown could object to requests for disclosure, or the requirement that a witness answer certain questions, on the basis that disclosure would be contrary to the public interest, or that the information was a Cabinet secret. If it belonged to the former category, the court would adjudicate the claim, balancing the public's general interest in disclosure with the specific public interest at issue in the claim for protection. One of the possible grounds of public interest was that "the disclosure would be injurious to international relations or national defence or security."[47] A considerable body of case law had evolved over time, and it tended to demonstrate less deference toward the government executive when balancing these interests (Stewart 2001: 219).

If the information belonged in the second category (a Cabinet secret), the Clerk of the Privy Counsel for Canada could issue a certificate, pursuant to section 39 of the *Canada Evidence Act*, declaring the information to be a Cabinet confidence, and the assertion was beyond review. It was an extraordinary power, but was limited to Cabinet secrets.[48]

Bill C-36 amended sections 37 and 38 of the *Canada Evidence Act* in a number of ways. The former procedure for adjudicating claims of privilege is mostly intact in the new version of section 37, but it is now subject to the procedure contemplated in sections 38 to 38.16.[49] Those sections are meant to deal with two new and broader categories of privilege: "potentially injurious information," which is defined as information that, if disclosed, "could injure international relations or national defence or national security"; and "sensitive information," which is defined as information "relating to international relations or national defence or national security that is in the possession of the Government of Canada, whether originating from inside or outside Canada, and is of a type that the Government of Canada is taking measures to safeguard." It is worth noting that on second reading of Bill C-36 (October 16th), Anne McLellan, justified these amendments by stating: "The Canada Evidence Act would be amended to allow for better protection of sensitive information during legal proceedings. One of the key reasons we need this improved protection is to be able to assure our allies that sensitive information they provide to us can be protected from release."[50]

In the former version of the Act, the government official involved in a proceeding was the person responsible for asserting privilege. This is also the case in the new scheme, but in addition, "participants" in proceedings, whoever they may be, now have a positive obligation to bring to the attention of the Attorney General (or the Crown) the fact that they believe they possess sensitive or potentially injurious information that may be disclosed, or that they are seeking to have disclosed.[51] A person possessing such information is prohibited from disclosing that information except in accordance with the scheme set out in the section.[52] Hamish Stewart has argued that this obligation is "remarkable," because

> virtually everyone connected with a proceeding would have a positive obligation to be aware of the nature of the information he or she might disclose and to notify the Attorney General of Canada of any possible disclosure. It is unclear how 'participants' are to be made aware of their obligations; whether there is any sanction for failure to discharge the obligation; and how the obligation relates to other obligations in the trial process, such as the Crown's constitutional duty of disclosure in criminal prosecutions, or the accused's constitutional right to solicitor-client privilege. (2003: 223)

It remains unclear what sanction could be imposed for a failure to notify the state of sensitive information, or to disclose sensitive information that one actually should have known was not to be disclosed. But it seems clear that the provision could be easily violated without intending to do so, or without even being aware of the fact.

If the Crown or a party other than the Crown is in possession of potentially injurious or sensitive information, an application can be made for its disclosure under sections 38.04 to 38.06. An application to protect information can also be made by the Crown. In either case, any hearing relating to section 38 must be held *in camera*, or in a hearing closed to the public. Where the Crown seeks to protect information, it can apply and be heard in the absence of the party affected. The Chief Justice of the Federal Court or a judge she or he designates has exclusive jurisdiction over the process, which means a distinct set of proceedings must begin if the matter arises out of one already in progress — for instance, in a criminal trial in a provincial superior court. The test for disclosure is found in 38.06, which allows the court, but does not require it, to disclose information if the court concludes that it is sensitive or would be injurious. If the court concludes that the information falls within either of these categories, it can still be disclosed if conditions can be crafted that "are most likely to limit any injury to international relations... or national security" and the court decides that "the public interest in disclosure outweighs in importance the public interest in non-disclosure."[53]

If the court has considered a matter under section 37 or 38 and decides that information should be disclosed, the Attorney General of Canada has an unusual power under section 38.13 to issue a certificate that effectively trumps the decision of the court. In earlier drafts of the bill, the issuance of a certificate under this section marked the end of the process. But this aspect of the scheme provoked considerable criticism by a number of commentators, including Stewart (2001) and Roach (2001). The final version of the bill subjects the Crown's certificate to what Roach has called a "light form of judicial review" by a single judge in the Federal Court of Appeal (2007: 7).[54] The test on appeal is whether any of the information has been "obtained in confidence from, or in relation to, a foreign entity... or [whether it relates to] national defence or national security."[55] The certificate can be varied, cancelled or upheld — whatever decision is made is final.[56] For Stewart,

> Sections 38.13 and 38.131 as enacted represent an improvement over the earlier version. But the right of appeal is still extremely limited, both institutionally and in the scope of the grounds. It is not the person presiding over the proceeding who makes the decision either to issue the certificate or to vary or cancel the certificate; indeed these sections apply only after the person presiding *and* a judge of the Federal Court, Trial Division have done whatever they can do. Furthermore, the new provisions still provide no mechanism for correcting any error by the Attorney General in assessing the balance between the interests in non-disclosure. In short, under ss. 38.13 and 38.131 the Attorney General is permitted to second-guess the outcome of a proceeding to which he was a party. (2003: 255)

The state has, in effect, the last word on what will be kept secret in any matter relating to national security.

Another significant and novel feature of the new scheme worth noting is the inclusion of companion sections 37.3 and 38.14, headed "protection of right to a fair trial." In essence, these sections state that if the court decides that information cannot be disclosed, or a certificate has been issued under 38.13 that impairs the right of the accused to a fair trial, the court can dismiss counts on an indictment, make a finding against the party asserting privilege, or even order a stay of proceedings.[57] Stewart argued that these sections add nothing to the court's jurisdiction to grant remedies under section 24(1) of the Charter. He also fears that these sections do not "[go] far enough to satisfy the trial right protected by s. 7 of the Charter, in that [they] subordinate the accused's right to a fair trial to the [new] disclosure regime" (2003: 221). But this argument might be qualified in two respects.

First, precisely because the general remedy provision in section 24(1) of the Charter is sufficiently broad, a remedy could be granted to the accused to prevent his or her section 7 rights from being subordinated. That is, a court could exercise its power under section 24(1) in the same way under both the old and new scheme. Second, Stewart underestimates the significance of including an explicit direction to judges to consider the otherwise extraordinary remedy of a judicial stay of proceedings in this context. By presenting the remedy to judges within the provisions that set out the scheme, Parliament is, in effect, suggesting to judges that, while judicial stays are considered extraordinary, including under the Charter, they are to be considered less extraordinary in this context.

But as both Kent Roach and Kathy Grant have pointed out, the wide discretion afforded to judges under this scheme can work both ways. Grant has expanded on Roach's comment that a dispute between a court and a Crown prosecutor over a question of privilege may well result in a stay of proceedings if the court takes the view that a violation of the right to a fair trial is more serious in that case than the nature of the crime in question (2003: 159). Grant has suggested that "while incredulous, the interests of justice in a case such as murder or terrorism might tip the balance in favour of proceeding in an unfair trial rather than ordering a judicial stay. There is a real possibility that trial judges, responding to the changing values of society, would prefer in [terrorism] cases to proceed with a trial that may be borderline unfair" (2003: 159).

The new scheme is certainly unusual and may well have the practical effect of expanding the scope of government privilege, or, as Grant has suggested, of lowering the threshold of the Crown's duty to disclose (2003: 167). However, the two features noted — judicial review of the Crown's power to issue a "secrecy certificate" and the remedy provisions to protect fair trial rights — arguably bring this set of amendments in Bill C-36 in closer conformity with the Charter. Stewart is sceptical on this point:

> it might be held that Bill C-36 infringes s. 7, with the Crown having to establish a justification under s. 1. I think that such a justification would be very hard to make out. Quite apart from the fact that the Supreme Court has never upheld a s. 7 breach under s. 1, Bill C-36 does not satisfy all the elements of the *Oakes* test. The restrictions on disclosure undoubtedly have a pressing and substantial objective and are rationally connected... but where the right to a fair trial could be protected by not trying the accused, i.e., through a stay of proceedings entered either by the Crown or by the court, it is hard to see how a refusal to disclose material relevant to making full answer and defence could be a minimal impairment of the fair trial right. (2003: 258)

Grant concurs and has argued that the *Canada Evidence Act* amendments in Bill C-36 would fail the "minimal impairment" portion of the *Oakes* test because "there are no effective limits on prosecutorial discretion to prohibit disclosure." She also took issue with the indefinite nature of these amendments and asked, "if the law is part of the 'War on Terror' should not the law only impair rights while the war is being fought? If the War on Terror is a permanent war, then the provisions cease to be extraordinary and the problem of being overbroad becomes more serious" (2003: 263).

The more critical point, however, is whether, even if the powers of the state could be restrained in some acceptable way, the changes to the *Canada Evidence Act* will, over the long run, result in a normalization of a deeper shift in our thinking about privilege. The Federal Court in 2007 found the requirement that all section 38 hearings be heard *in camera* violated the freedom of expression in section 2 of the Charter, and could not be justified under section 1.[58] But two months later, in an application for disclosure in *Khawaja*, the same court found that the Crown's ability to apply for privilege in the absence of the affected party does not violate the Charter.[59]

A number of questions about section 38 therefore remain. If it is acceptable to allow the government to make extraordinary demands on "participants," and to give the government what amounts to a final decision over what will remain privileged, one has to ask where will the process end? If it becomes acceptable to build into the law so many protections for state secrets — and to make it easier to assert privilege over something as nebulous as "national security" (a term not defined in any federal legislation) — at what point will the principle of a "full and fair trial" begin to mean something altogether different?

Conclusion

> When the State turns to its power to investigate, detain, punish and imprison, the standard of justification should be high, even in extraordinary times. Basic principles of a criminal justice system that deserves the name require the state to prove both that the individual acted and was at fault, that responsibility be fairly labeled and that any punishment be proportionate to the accused's actions. (Stuart 2003: 154)

The intended effect of focusing on these sections of Bill C-36 is to demonstrate that the *Anti-Terrorism Act* implies a significant departure from what Don Stuart, in the passage above, calls the "basic principles of a criminal justice system" (2003: 154). The common assumption in these sections is that an accused terror suspect or group is too dangerous to be afforded the presumption of innocence or protections of due process found in conventional criminal cases. The fear of terrorism, and a belief in the need for extraordinary measures, justifies an approach in which the accused terrorist is dealt with under a new set of guiding principles or a qualified interpretation of earlier ones.

The *Anti-Terrorism Act* might have been passed temporarily; had this been done, lawmakers and legal commentators might have spent less time fretting about whether and how the Act's provisions were consistent with principles that have conventionally guided the administration of justice. However, given the indefinite change to Canadian law made by all but two of these amendments, and the government's claim that they are consistent with the Constitution, a more probing and contentious debate was bound to take place. It should suffice to say at this stage of the argument that the course taken by Parliamentarians in the fall of 2001 was determined in part by features unique to our constitutional law and structure. That course also helped to shape a new perspective on the administration of justice in which departures from earlier principles and concepts would seem necessary and justified. In the next chapter, we explore ways in which the path forged by Parliament was soon followed by the judiciary.

Notes

1. President Bush's state of emergency was issued on September 14, 2001, in "Proc. 7463, Declaration of National Emergency by Reason of Certain Terrorist Attacks." The government of the United Kingdom invoked a state of emergency on November 13, 2001. Available at: <http://observer.guardian.co.uk/international/story/0,6903,591394,00.html> (accessed on February 8, 2008).
2. This order is found online at: <http://www.whitehouse.gov/news/releases/2001/11/20011113-27.html> (accessed on February 8, 2008).
3. See, for example, *Rasul v. Bush*, 542 U.S. 466 (2004), a decision recognizing the right of non-national detainees to challenge their detention on the grounds of the doctrine of "wrongful imprisonment"; *Hamdi v. Rumsfeld*, 542 U.S. 507 (2004), recognizing the right of only those detainees with U.S. citizenship to challenge their detention by *habeas corpus*; and *Hamdan v. Rumsfeld*, 548 U.S. (2006), successfully challenging the validity of the military tribunals set up to try detainees.
4. See, for example, Ronald Dworkin, "The Threat to Patriotism," *New York Review of Books*, v. 49, no. 3, February 28, 2002; "Terror and the Attack on Civil Liberties," *New York Review of Books*, v. 50, no. 17, November 6, 2003; "What the Court Really Said," *New York Review of Books*, v. 51, no. 13, August 12, 2004.
5. *Uniting and Strengthening America by Providing Appropriate Tools Required To Intercept and Obstruct Terrorism (USA PATRIOT) Act of 2001*, Pub. L. No. 107-56, 115 Stat. 272, 276 (2001).
6. *Terrorism Act, 2000*, Acts of the U.K. Parliament, 2000, c. 11.
7. Acts of the U.K. Parliament, 2001, c. 24.
8. Part 4 the 2001 Act.
9. *A (FC) and Others (FC) v. SSHD*, [2004] UKHL 56.
10. The *Prevention of Terrorism Act*, U.K., 2005, c. 2; the *Terrorism Act*, U.K., 2006, c. 11.
11. The editorial is cited by Dyzenhaus (2001: 22).
12. S.C. 2001, c. 41.
13. See Canada, Parliament, House of Commons, 37th Parliament, 1st Session: *House of Commons Debates (Hansard)*, October 16 to 18 and November 27 and 28, 2001; available at: <http://www2.parl.gc.ca/housechamberbusiness/chamberindex.aspx?View=H&Parl=37&Ses=1&File=t-37-1_2-e.

htm&Language=E&Mode=1> (last accessed February 8, 2008).

14. Ibid.
15. See, for example, the 1996 Constitution of South Africa, or the European *Convention on Human Rights*, cited in the Introduction.
16. S.C. 1988, c. 29.
17. Sections 58 and 59 provide for a Parliamentary committee to assess the validity of a declaration of emergency made under the Act and the power to revoke it.
18. For an excellent overview of the enacted version of Bill C-36 see Kent Roach, "Criminalizing Terrorism" in *September 11: Consequences for Canada* (McGill-Queens U P: Montreal, 2003). See also submissions to Parliamentary committees in 2001 and 2005 by the Canadian Bar Association, the British Columbia Civil Liberties Association, and the Canadian Association of University Teachers; these are available online at: <http://www.cba.org/CBA/submissions/Main/>, <http://www.bccla.org/05antiterror.htm>, and <http://www.caut.ca/en/issues/civil_liberties/Default.asp> (last accessed February 8, 2008).
19. R.S. 1985, c. C-46.
20. The definition of "terrorism offence" appears in section 2 of the *Code* and includes "an indictable offence under this or any other Act of Parliament where the act or omission constituting the offence also constitutes a terrorist activity."
21. Court file: 04-G30282.
22. For the full text of the counts charged, see *R. v. Khawaja*, [2006] C.C.S. No. 12212, [2006] O.J. No. 4245.
23. Ibid. at paragraph 3.
24. Ibid. at paragraph 18.
25. Ibid. at paragraph 24.
26. Ibid. at paragraphs 39-40.
27. Ibid. at paragraph 58.
28. The court applied the test for a section 1 analysis set out in *R. v. Oakes*, [1986] 1 S.C.R. 103.
29. Ibid.
30. Bill S-3, 39th Parliament — 2nd Session, 2007.
31. Section 83.3 of the *Criminal Code*.
32. Section 83.28 of the *Criminal Code*.
33. Section 83.28(5)(e).
34. See the discussion of *Vancouver Sun (Re)*, [2004] 2 S.C.R. 332 in Chapter 2.
35. *R. v. Malik and Bagri*, 2005 BCSC 350.
36. *Re Application Under s. 83.28 of the Criminal Code*, [2004] 2 S.C.R. 248
37. From the headnote.
38. Ibid. Bill C-36 amends the *National Defence Act*, R.S., 1985, c. N-5, by adding sections 273.65 and 273.69.
39. Sections 273.65(1) and (3) of the *National Defence Act*.
40. Section 83.05, which sets out the scheme for a list of terrorist entities, points back to the definition of "terrorist group" in section 83.01(1) of the *Criminal Code*.
41. Section 83.05 provides for the creation of a list and section 83.18 addresses "participating, facilitating, instructing and harbouring" in the activities of a

"terrorist group."

42. See sections 83.05(1) and (1.1) of the *Criminal Code*.

43. See sections 278.2(2) and 278.5(1) of the *Criminal Code*.

44. These provisions withstood a Charter challenge in *R v. Mills*, [1999] 3 S.C.R. 668.

45. R.S.C. 1985, c. C-5.

46. For this portion of the chapter, I draw extensively upon Hamish Stewart (2001 and 2003), Peter Rosenthal (2003), and Kathy Grant (2003).

47. Ibid. 220; see the former section 37(1). An attempt to assert privilege on that ground could be adjudicated only by the Chief Justice of the Federal Court, or his or her designate (see the former section 37(2)).

48. Ibid. see the former section 39.

49. Section 37(1) *Canada Evidence Act*.

50. See Canada, Parliament, House of Commons, 37th Parliament, 1st Session: *House of Commons Debates (Hansard)*, October 16 to 18 and November 27 and 28th, 2001; available at: <http://www2.parl.gc.ca/housechamberbusiness/chamberindex.aspx?View=H&Parl=37&Ses=1&File=t-37-1_2-e.htm&Language=E&Mode=1> (last accessed February 8, 2008).

51. Section 38.01(1) and (2) *Canada Evidence Act*.

52. Section 38.02(1) *Canada Evidence Act*.

53. Section 38.06(2) *Canada Evidence Act*.

54. Section 38.131 *Canada Evidence Act*.

55. Section 38.131(8)-(10) *Canada Evidence Act*.

56. Section 38.131(11) *Canada Evidence Act*.

57. This is set out in subsection (2) of 37.3 and 38.14 *Canada Evidence Act*.

58. *Toronto Star v. Canada*, [2007] F.C. 128.

59. *Khawaja*, [2007] F.C. 463.

Chapter 2

The Courts and Section 7
after September 11th

Turning in this chapter from Parliament to the courts, we shift focus from the *Anti-Terrorism Act* as an object of contention to the meaning of the phrase "fundamental justice" in section 7 of the *Charter of Rights*. As courts begin to address the validity of counter-terrorism law more frequently, the protection of "life, liberty and security of the person" in section 7 becomes central to the debate. In the last chapter, we saw how sections of the Act could be used to investigate and prosecute suspects in ways that diverge from conventional approaches to the administration of justice. In this chapter, we explore three cases where judges have grappled with core constitutional principles in the context of terrorism. In each of the cases, the court has sought to justify significant departures from guiding principles as necessary measures in an evolving national security mandate, and has also found such measures consistent with "fundamental justice."

The Supreme Court of Canada's decisions in *Suresh v. Canada*,[1] *Re: Application under s. 83.28 of the Criminal Code*,[2] and *Charkaoui v. Canada*[3] each engage the question of the constitutional rights of terrorist suspects — and in particular the application of section 7 of the Charter.[4] The *Suresh* decision assesses the scope of the Charter's protection against deportation where there is a substantial risk of facing torture; the second decision concerns the validity of the investigative hearing provisions in the *Anti-Terrorism Act* discussed in the previous chapter; and the final decision addresses the constitutional validity of the "security certificate" regime under Canada's *Immigration and Refugee Protection Act*.[5] This regime allows members of the executive to order the detention, indeterminate imprisonment, and eventual deportation of any non-citizen believed to be a threat to national security.

In each of these cases, the court's analysis of whether the appellant's section 7 rights have been breached involves a "balancing" of individual and state interests. A balancing at this stage allows the court, in some of these cases, to avoid a finding that fundamental rights have been breached. With no breach, there is no need to consider whether deportation to torture, or other undesirable measures, are justified as reasonable limits to rights in section 1 of the Charter — the section setting out general limits to rights. As Parliament had done earlier, courts in these cases could find that by virtue of a balancing of interests, unjust measures could still be consistent with Charter rights — and thus, still be "constitutional." This balancing has also led to the perverse result of finding extraordinary, unjust, and inhumane measures consistent with what are called the "principles of fundamental justice" in the Charter.

But this, and other aspects of the application of section 7 in terrorism cases, remains a matter of contention among the judiciary. Dissenting opinions and reversals by higher courts point to a divide between a jurisprudence that finds certain measures necessary and therefore justified, and one that finds that the practice of counter-terrorism entailed by these measures is moving too far away from core principles and ideals of the justice system. To understand these developments in context, it would be useful to look first at section 7 of the Charter and how courts had set out to apply it in earlier cases.

The Principles of Fundamental Justice

Section 7 states: "Everyone has the right to life, liberty and security of the person and the right not to be deprived thereof except in accordance with the principles of fundamental justice." The question that first arises is: what exactly is meant by the latter part of the sentence? The Supreme Court of Canada answered this question in a 1985 case, *Re B.C. Motor Vehicle Act*,[6] that serves as a starting point for the judicial interpretation of "fundamental justice," and sets out a basic model for a constitutional challenge based on section 7.

The government of British Columbia had asked the court in that case to render an opinion on the constitutional validity of a recent amendment of its *Motor Vehicle Act*. Section 94 of the Act made "driving while prohibited" or driving without a valid licence an absolute liability offence. A person could be found guilty and sentenced to prison without having actually known, at the time, that he or she was in fact a prohibited driver, or lacked a valid licence. A person could therefore be found guilty and imprisoned despite the possibility of an innocent explanation. The British Columbia Court of Appeal found the provision contrary to section 7 and not justified under section 1, and the Supreme Court agreed.

Writing for a majority of the Court, then Justice Lamer set out the Court's first substantial judicial interpretation of the phrase "principles of fundamental justice": two important points emerged from his analysis. The first was that the Court rejected the Attorney General's argument that "fundamental justice" should be interpreted restrictively to refer to procedural as opposed to substantive content.[7] Although there was some indication that the Charter's drafters believed "fundamental justice" to be synonymous with "natural justice," Lamer opted instead to look at section 7 in the context of the Charter as a whole. Citing the Court's recent decision in *Hunter v. Southam*,[8] he proposed to read section 7 with the broader purposes of the Charter in mind, considering the rights intended to be protected in the section.[9] The difference between the two approaches (procedural and substantive) is that, if fundamental justice were to refer to procedural or natural justice, the right to "life, liberty and security of the person" could be easily addressed by providing only for certain procedural protections, such as an impartial tribunal, or an opportunity to be heard. The obvious danger, as Lamer pointed out, is that "the narrower the meaning given to 'principles of fundamental justice' the greater will be the possibility that individuals may be deprived of these most basic rights."[10]

The second point was that the best indication of how to read the phrase "principles of fundamental justice" was to be found in the Charter itself:

> Sections 8 to 14 are illustrative of deprivations of those rights to life, liberty and security of the person in breach of the principles of fundamental justice. For they, in effect, illustrate some of the parameters of the "right" to life, liberty and security of the person; they are examples of instances in which the "right" to life, liberty and security of the person would be violated in a manner which is not in accordance with the principles of fundamental justice. To put matters in a different way, ss. 7 to 14 could have been fused into one section, with inserted between the words of s. 7 and the rest of those sections the oft utilised provision in our statutes, "and, without limiting the generality of the foregoing (s. 7) the following shall be deemed to be in violation of a person's rights under this section." Clearly, some of those sections embody principles that are beyond what could be characterized as "procedural."[11]

It is important to note, however, that sections 8 to 14 — the ones that set out specific "legal rights," such as the right to counsel, the right to be free from unreasonable search and seizure, the right to a trial within a reasonable time, and so on — are merely illustrative for Lamer of the possible content of fundamental justice; they are not exhaustive. But while the phrase "fundamental justice" remains open-ended, it should also be seen in the context of a broader tradition:

> ["Fundamental justice"] represent[s] principles which have been recognized by the common law, the international conventions and by the very fact of entrenchment in the Charter, as essential elements of a system for the administration of justice which is founded upon the belief in the dignity and worth of the human person and the rule of law.[12]

After setting out what the phrase "principles of fundamental justice" might mean, Justice Lamer then considered what should happen when the Court does find that a law violates the principles of fundamental justice. The section under review in this case violated these principles because the "fundamental principles of penal liability" have long held that it is repugnant to send a "morally innocent" person to prison.[13] In other words, in order to incarcerate a person, the Crown should have to prove both the *mens rea* and the *actus reus* of the offence (or the element of intent along with the physical fact of its having been committed). But having decided this point, Lamer was clear that the focus of the analysis should then turn to section 1 — to determine whether the violation of section 7 constitutes a reasonable limit. The Attorney General's strongest argument in favour of allowing for absolute liability in this context was "administrative expediency." Lamer made clear why this argument should be addressed at the section 1 stage and not section 7:

> Administrative expediency, absolute liability's main supportive argument, will undoubtedly under s. 1 be invoked and occasionally succeed. Indeed, administrative expediency certainly has its place in administrative law. But when administrative law chooses to call in aid imprisonment through penal law, indeed sometimes criminal law and the added stigma attached to a conviction, exceptional, in my view, will be the case where the liberty or even the security of the person guaranteed under s. 7 should be sacrificed to administrative expediency. Section 1 may, for reasons of administrative expediency, successfully come to the rescue of an otherwise violation of s. 7, but only in cases arising out of exceptional conditions, such as natural disasters, the outbreak of war, epidemics, and the like.[14]

The issue at the section 7 stage is, therefore, not whether a law violates a principle of fundamental justice but is justifiable nonetheless; it is strictly a question of whether a violation has been made out. Justifications — including the balancing of individual with societal or state interests — belong in section 1.

Justice Lamer also addressed the issue of who bears the burden of proof. Whereas at the section 7 stage, the accused has the burden of proving there has been a breach of his or her rights, at the section 1 stage, the burden shifts to the Crown to prove the breach is justified in a "free and democratic society." In this case, the state failed to meet the burden, because it failed to establish why a strict liability regime (allowing for a defence of having taken reasonable precautions, i.e., "due diligence") would not have been equally effective or expedient in terms of the province's objectives.[15] Notably, it was Lamer's sense that if something like national security was the issue, the justification of a violation of "life, liberty and security of the person" should take place after acknowledging that those rights had been violated and moving on to the framework of section 1.

In what follows, I will turn to three cases decided after September 11, 2001, in which almost all of these points are lost. The suggestion that courts should apply a "purposive interpretation" is forgotten; a justification of a deprivation of life, liberty and security of the person takes place at the section 7 stage instead of at section 1; and, by virtue of that fact, a breach of fundamental justice no longer requires exceptional circumstances to be justified. This is not, however, the beginning of a trend on the part of the Court. The migration of the "justification" analysis from section 1 to section 7 in Supreme Court jurisprudence can be traced back at least as far as the *Rodriguez* decision (1993), which is beyond the scope of this chapter.[16] What is notable here is how much more important this interpretive strategy has become in the context of terrorism. For reasons that will become clear below, the desire to engage in a justification at the section 7 stage follows from a desire to avoid having to concede that fundamental principles have been violated, or having to finesse the more contentious question of whether such violations can be justified in a "free and democratic society."

Justifying Torture

The case of Manickavasagam Suresh reached the Supreme Court of Canada in May of 2001, but the Court's decision was rendered in January of 2002. A cursory reading of this unanimous decision suggests that it deals mostly with technical and procedural aspects of the Minister of Citizenship and Immigration's decision to deport a refugee who fears that he may face torture if returned to Sri Lanka. But on a closer reading, it is in fact a significant statement of the Court's position on human rights in terrorism cases. It amounts to a declaration that when dealing with a suspected terrorist, even the most fundamental of human rights — the right not to be tortured — is not absolutely protected in Canadian law, but is instead to be balanced with the interests of "national security." In an extraordinary show of deference to government, the Court ruled that the question of whether the balance has been struck correctly, in any given case, is one the courts are content to defer to the Minister her or himself.

Suresh was a Sri Lankan refugee whom the Canadian Security and Intelligence Service (CSIS) believed to be a member of, and fundraiser for, a group known as the "Liberation Tigers of Tamil Eelam." The Canadian government believed this group to be involved in terrorism, but also knew that members of the group had been tortured in Sri Lanka.[17] Suresh was detained in 1995 as a security risk and deportation proceedings began under the *Immigration Act*.[18]

Suresh challenged many parts of the Act. Although the Act was replaced in 2002 with the *Immigration and Refugee Protection Act*, the deportation scheme and much of the language in the provisions discussed in this case remain the same. Section 53(1) of the earlier Act stated that no one found to be a Convention refugee can be removed from Canada to "a country where the person's life or freedom would be threatened for reasons of race, religion, nationality, membership in a particular social group or political opinion unless... the person is a member of an inadmissible class... and the Minister is of the opinion that the person constitutes a danger to the security of Canada." Section 19 defined the inadmissible class as including, among others, persons "who there are reasonable grounds to believe... are members of an organization that there are reasonable grounds to believe will... engage in terrorism" — or have done so in the past. The section excludes persons who have "satisfied the Minister that their admission would not be detrimental to the national interest." Section 40.1 of the Act provided for the issuance of what is called a "security certificate." The Minister of Immigration and the Solicitor General of Canada could issue one when the two form the opinion that a person, other than a Canadian citizen or a permanent resident, is a person described in section 19.[19] (In the updated version of the Act, anyone who is not a citizen can be subject to a security certificate.) Once issued, the certificate acts as a warrant for the detention of the person named in it. The detainee can challenge the validity of the certificate —— that is, the detainee can seek review of whether the Minister and Solicitor General's opinions giving rise to the issuance of the certificate were "reasonable."[20] If the Court defers to the opinion of the Minister and Solicitor General, deportation proceedings begin.

In this case, the review hearing of the security certificate in Federal Court took some fifty days.[21] At the conclusion of that hearing, Justice Teitelbaum found the certificate to be reasonable, but also made other key findings. Suresh had been a member of the group in question; the group had been involved in terrorist activities; and some members of the group had been subject to torture by the Sri Lankan government. The matter then went before an immigration adjudicator to decide whether Suresh should be deported. The adjudicator found that there was no reason to believe Suresh had been directly involved in terrorism, but should be deported on the basis of his membership in a terrorist organization (in accordance with section 19).[22] The adjudicator also recommended that the Minister issue an opinion under section 53(1)(b) of the Act that Suresh constituted a danger to the security of Canada and should be deported. The Minister promptly provided this opinion.

The adjudicator, however, made the recommendation without providing Suresh with a copy of his memorandum to the Minister and without giving Suresh an opportunity to respond to the assertions it contained.[23] The adjudicator stated that Suresh "is not known to have personally committed any acts of violence either in Canada or Sri Lanka" and that his conduct in Canada was "non-violent."[24] The adjudicator also conceded that Suresh was at risk if returned to Sri Lanka, but took the view that the risk was "difficult to assess; might be tempered by his high profile; and was counterbalanced by Suresh's terrorist activities in Canada."[25] Suresh sought judicial review of the Minister's section 53 opinion: he argued that it was unreasonable and the result of an unfair process (involving the adjudicator's memo), and that it violated section 7 and section 2 (the right to freedom of association, and being a danger to Canada on the basis of being a member of a terrorist organization) of the Charter.

It is notable that Suresh's Charter challenge on the grounds of both section 2 and section 7 failed in the Federal Court, the Federal Court of Appeal, and eventually, the Supreme Court. Justice Robertson of the Federal Court of Appeal found that not only was section 7 not violated by the prospect of Suresh being deported to face torture, but that the right under international law not to be tortured was not absolute. It was limited, rather, by a nation's right to deport those who threaten national security.[26] The Supreme Court of Canada's review of the case yielded only a slight adjustment to the remarkable tenor of this line of reasoning: international law may recognize no limits to the prohibition against torture, but Canadian law does. For reasons that will become clear, the Supreme Court's section 7 analysis in *Suresh* entails a significant shift from both international law norms and earlier approaches to the protection of human rights in the Charter.

The reading of section 7 conducted by Canada's highest court is framed by the question, "Does the Act permit deportation to torture contrary to the Charter?"[27] The issue in this case was whether a deportation under section 53(1)(b) would be contrary to the "principles of fundamental justice." On the content of that key phrase, the Court stated:

> Deportation to torture... requires us to consider a variety of factors,

including the circumstances or conditions of the potential deportee, the danger that the deportee presents to Canadians or the country's security, and the threat of terrorism to Canada....

Determining whether deportation to torture violates the principles of fundamental justice requires us to balance Canada's interest in combating terrorism and the Convention refugee's interest in not being deported to torture. Canada has a legitimate and compelling interest in combating terrorism. But it is also committed to fundamental justice. The notion of proportionality is fundamental to our constitutional system. Thus we must ask whether the government's proposed response is reasonable in relation to the threat. In the past, we have held that some responses are so extreme that they are per se disproportionate to any legitimate government interest: see *Burns* [i.e., *United States v. Burns*[28]]. We must ask whether deporting a refugee to torture would be such a response.[29]

The tone of these paragraphs belies the significance of what they assert. When the Court states that "the approach is essentially one of balancing," it is contemplating the justification of forcing a person to face torture. As has been mentioned above, the courts have undertaken a balancing of social and individual interests at the section 7 stage in earlier cases, but with less striking results, and for different purposes.

We might pause momentarily to appreciate the differences by looking briefly at the Court's analysis of "fundamental justice" in earlier cases dealing with deportation to face the possibility of the death penalty. The "balancing" contemplated in *Burns*, for example, was entirely different from what is contemplated in *Suresh*. *Burns* concerned the plight of two eighteen-year-old Canadians charged with murders that took place in Washington State. If extradited back to Washington, the case could result in the death penalty. The Minister's authority under the *Extradition Act* to render the accused in this case depended on the interpretation of powers under this Act.[30] Since the treaty provided the Minister with some discretion as to whether to grant an extradition order, the Minister had taken the position that it was not necessary in absolutely every case to seek an assurance that the death penalty would not be imposed before granting an order. The question for the Court was whether the Minister's discretion was limited by section 7 of the Charter: specifically, whether the Charter required the Minister to seek the assurance in every extradition case. Notably, the Court found that given the nature of the case (an extreme deprivation of "life, liberty and security of the person"), it was appropriate to be less deferential to ministerial discretion:

We affirm that it is generally for the Minister, not the Court, to assess the weight of competing considerations in extradition policy, but the availability of the death penalty, like death itself, opens up a different dimension. The difficulties and occasional miscarriages of the criminal law are located in an area of human experience that falls squarely within "the inherent domain of the judiciary as guardian of the justice system": *Re B.C. Motor Vehicle Act*.... It is from this perspective, recognizing the unique finality and irreversibility of the death penalty, that the constitutionality of the Minister's decision falls to be decided.[31]

And with respect to the application of section 7 specifically, the Court took a critical view of earlier jurisprudence:

> Our analysis will lead to the conclusion that *in the absence of exceptional circumstances*, which we refrain from trying to anticipate, assurances in death penalty cases are always constitutionally required. [Emphasis added.]

The Court appeared to leave open the possibility of an exception while gesturing in the direction of absolute protection against the death penalty — moving away from the position set out in earlier decisions on point, *Kindler v. Canada (Minister of Justice)*[32] and *Reference re Ng Extradition (Can.)*.[33] The issue in both of these cases was the same as in *Burns*: whether the Minister's decision to extradite the appellants to face the possibility of the death penalty without seeking assurances that they would not be executed was contrary to the principles of fundamental justice. In both cases, the majority found that it was not contrary, because, in essence, it would not "shock the conscience" of Canadians to learn that the accused in these cases were being extradited for this purpose, and because taking an absolute stand in favour of assurances could lead to Canada becoming a "safe heaven" for murderers. The Court retreats from this position in *Burns*:

> Even though the rights of the fugitive are to be considered in the context of other applicable principles of fundamental justice, which are normally of sufficient importance to uphold the extradition, a particular treatment or punishment may sufficiently violate our sense of fundamental justice as to tilt the balance against extradition. Examples might include stoning to death individuals taken in adultery, or lopping off the hands of a thief. The punishment is so extreme that it becomes the controlling issue in the extradition and overwhelms the rest of the analysis. The respondents contend that now, unlike perhaps in 1991 when *Kindler* and *Ng* were decided, capital punishment is *the* issue.[34]

This is tantamount, in other words, to the proposition that "our sense of fundamental justice" is intimately related to the extremity of abuse: if the abuse is sufficiently extreme, it can "overwhelm" the analysis. In other words, it may be possible to balance factors, but when it is clear that a person would suffer unspeakable harm, fundamental justice is violated. Whether the violation could be justified by other considerations is a question that is reserved for section 1.

In *Burns*, the Court proceeds to weigh factors "for and against" extradition without assurances and it balances these as a part of its analysis of whether extradition to face the death penalty is in accordance with "fundamental justice." The Court concludes that fundamental justice favours extradition only with assurances, and the violation of section 7 cannot be justified under section 1 in this case, because "[w]hile the government objective of advancing mutual assistance in the fight against crime is entirely legitimate, the Minister has not shown that extraditing the respondents to face the death penalty without assurances is necessary to achieve that objective."[35] But the Court includes this exception:

> Nevertheless, we do not foreclose the possibility that there may be situations where the Minister's objectives are so pressing, and where there is no other way to achieve those objectives other than through extradition without assurances, that a violation might be justified. In this case, we find no such justification.[36]

The exception therefore functions differently in *Burns* and *Suresh*. Whereas in *Burns*, extreme harm is simply contrary to fundamental justice, in *Suresh*, it may not be. In *Burns*, a person could be extradited without an assurance if the extraordinary Ministerial objective were appropriate under section 1; while in *Suresh*, the balancing exercise in section 7 would, in exceptional circumstances, justify actual torture in the name of some national security concern. The difference may be technical, but it leads to the perverse result that in the one case, a person would be extradited without being executed; in the other case, a person would be tortured to make Canada safer. The Court comes much closer to providing an absolute prohibition against extradition to face the death penalty, in the one case, than it does to providing an absolute prohibition against deportation to face torture in the other.[37]

To resume, then, with the analysis of section 7 in *Suresh*, the next notable step in the Court's logic is to ask whether "from a Canadian perspective, returning a refugee to the risk of torture because of security concerns violates the principles of fundamental justice where the deportation is effected for reasons of national security."[38] The Court draws a comparison between deportation to torture in the present case and the problem of extradition to face the death penalty in *Burns* and concludes that both would be repugnant to the Canadian sensibility of "fundamental justice." Crucial to the analysis in this case, however, is a balancing of interests:

> Canadian jurisprudence does not suggest that Canada may never deport a person to face treatment elsewhere that would be unconstitutional if imposed by Canada directly, on Canadian soil. To repeat, the appropriate approach is essentially one of balancing. The outcome will depend not only on considerations inherent in the general context but also on considerations related to the circumstances and condition of the particular person whom the government seeks to expel. On the one hand stands the state's genuine interest in combating terrorism, preventing Canada from becoming a safe haven for terrorists, and protecting public security. On the other hand stands Canada's constitutional commitment to liberty and fair process. This said, Canadian jurisprudence suggests that this balance will usually come down against expelling a person to face torture elsewhere.[39]

Looking exclusively at domestic law, the Court concludes that, despite the social consensus against the use of torture here or elsewhere, in exceptional cases deportation to face the risk of torture could be consistent with "fundamental justice." In such a case, section 1 would never be considered.

The Court goes on to survey various international law instruments and treaties on the question of torture and asserts that these must be factored into the analysis of "fundamental justice." On the status of these principles, the Court states: "International treaty norms are not, strictly speaking, binding in Canada unless they have been incorporated into Canadian law by enactment. However, in seeking the meaning of the Canadian Constitution, the courts may be informed by international law."[40] The Court cites a list of international treaties that prohibit torture, including the *International Covenant on Civil and Political Rights* (1966), which Canada ratified in 1976.[41] Contrary to the findings of the Federal Court of Appeal, the Court here acknowledges that this and other international treaties absolutely prohibit deportation to torture, and do not allow for derogation from the prohibition where derogation clauses are included. The Court also notes that "the Supreme Court of Israel sitting as the High Court of Justice and the House of Lords have rejected torture as a legitimate tool to use in combating terrorism and protecting national security."[42] The Court then concludes:

> both domestic and international jurisprudence suggest that torture is so abhorrent that it will almost always be disproportionate to interests on the other side of the balance, even security interests. This suggests that, barring extraordinary circumstances, deportation to

> torture will generally violate the principles of fundamental justice
> protected by s. 7 of the Charter. [43]

Curiously, however, although the Court appears here to treat deportation to torture as "categorically" inconsistent with fundamental justice, it soon shifts, without explanation, to being "generally" inconsistent. The closest the Court comes to explaining this shift is the following:

> We do not exclude the possibility that in exceptional circumstances, deportation to face torture might be justified, either as a consequence of the balancing process mandated by s. 7 of the Charter or under s. 1…. [T]he fundamental justice balance under s. 7 of the Charter generally precludes deportation to torture when applied on a case-by-case basis. We may predict that it will rarely be struck in favour of expulsion where there is a serious risk of torture. However, as the matter is one of balance, precise prediction is elusive. The ambit of an exceptional discretion to deport to torture, if any, must await future cases. [44]

For these reasons, the Court finds that section 53(1)(b) does not violate section 7 of the Charter. In short, fundamental justice requires a balancing: in some cases, it is conceivable that the national security interest could outweigh a person's right not to face torture. Yet that kind of decision would still be consistent with "fundamental justice."

Investigative Hearings: A Constitutional Challenge

In the previous chapter, I reviewed the "investigative hearing" provisions of the *Anti-Terrorism Act*. These sections are the only part of the bill that has been subject to a Charter challenge, and that has reached the Supreme Court of Canada. Although the provisions have now lapsed, the decision in that case remains relevant in part because a bill has been tabled in the Senate in late 2007 that proposes to revive investigative hearings. [45] The decision is also relevant because the Court's reasoning, and in particular its balancing of the state's interest in national security with individual liberty, sheds light on how other parts of the *Anti-Terrorism Act* might be approached in future cases. At the least, the case stands as a record of the Court's own internal divide over the legitimacy of a significant experiment in Parliament's legislative counter-terror strategy: it strongly suggests the divide would extend well beyond this part of the Act.

Briefly, section 83.28 of the *Criminal Code* allows for Crown counsel to approve an application for, and a judge to grant, an order requiring a person who has not been charged with an offence to appear before the court for questioning with respect to a terrorism offence. By involving the court in the investigative stage of a matter, the "investigative hearing" diverges from the normal practice of allowing for compelled testimony only once charges have been laid, and only in the course of a trial or a preliminary hearing. Once an order is granted under section 83.28, the person named can be arrested, compelled to answer questions, and charged with contempt for refusing to testify or for providing false testimony. The section does preclude the use of the testimony in criminal proceedings against the person, except proceedings for contempt — but for reasons to be explored below, this does not amount to a guarantee against self-incrimination.

The decision in *(Re) Application under s. 83.28 of the Criminal Code* involved a peculiar resort to the investigative hearing provisions by Crown counsel in the course of the Air India trial. That case concerned a terrorist act committed in 1985, and proceeded in the form of a prosecution for first-degree murder.[46] The Crown sought to question a witness who had proved to be uncooperative: section 83.28 provided a means to compel the witness to attend for questioning under oath, before a judge. The provisions also allowed for the questioning to be conducted *in camera*, in the absence of defence counsel, and even without counsel's knowledge: incredibly, the questioning took place in the same Vancouver courthouse in which the Air India trial was taking place. By chance, a member of the defence team for one of the accused became aware of the hearing and, together with counsel for the co-accused, challenged the constitutional validity of the entire investigative hearing scheme. In a parallel matter, the *Vancouver Sun* newspaper sought access to the proceeding and challenged the closed nature of the hearing.

Both challenges were heard in short order by the Supreme Court of Canada, which rendered two decisions. On the question of the secrecy of the hearing, the Court found that a presumption of openness could be read into the provisions, and should therefore be provided. This rendered the hearing constitutional in that respect.[47] The challenge brought by the accused in the Air India trial advanced two main arguments. The scheme violated section 7 of the Charter — the right to liberty and to silence in a manner contrary to the principles of fundamental justice — and the principle of judicial independence. This principle was derived from section 11(d) of the Charter (which applies only to persons charged with an offence), but also from sections 96 to 100 of the *Constitution Act, 1867*.[48] The majority of the Court dismissed both arguments, arguing that the scheme was consistent with section 7, due to the various protections it contained, and that it did not violate the principle of judicial independence. But Justices LeBel and Fish vigorously expressed a dissenting opinion: they found that the scheme marked a significant departure from the traditional role of the judiciary, that it violated the principle of judicial independence, and that it was unconstitutional on that ground alone. An exploration of the reasons of both the majority and dissenting opinions in this case illustrates a significant gap in perspectives that points to a deeper divide over the legitimacy of certain departures from conventional principles in the fight against terror.

The majority's reasons in this case are dispersed in three opinions, one authored by Justices Iacobucci and Arbour (writing also for Chief Justice McLachlin and Justice Major), another by Justices Bastarache and Deschamps (agreeing with the decision of Iacobucci and Arbour, but expanding on the analysis briefly), and a third by Justice Binnie (noting that the section was constitutional but the purpose for which it was applied in this instance was improper). One key aspect of Iacobucci and Arbour's reasons provided at the outset of their analysis — and one that may become more important in future challenges to the Act — is their determination of the purpose of the *Anti-Terrorism Act*:

> It was suggested in submissions that the purpose of the Act should be regarded broadly as the protection of "national security." However, we believe that this characterization has the potential to go too far and would have implications that far outstrip legislative intent. The discussions surrounding the legislation, and the legislative language itself clearly demonstrate that the Act purports to provide means by which terrorism may be prosecuted and prevented. As we cautioned above, courts must not fall prey to the rhetorical urgency of a perceived emergency or an altered security paradigm. While the threat posed by terrorism is certainly more tangible in the aftermath of global events such as those perpetrated in the United States, and since then elsewhere, including very recently in Spain, we must not lose sight of the particular aims of the legislation. Notably, the Canadian government opted to enact specific criminal law and procedure legislation and did not make use of exceptional powers, for example under the *Emergencies Act...* or invoke the notwithstanding clause at s. 33 of the Charter.
>
> We conclude that the purpose of the Act is the prosecution and prevention of terrorism offences.[49]

The difference between national security and the prevention of terrorism as legislative goals is subtle, but significant. Interpreting the *Anti-Terrorism Act* to have this more restricted and less partial purpose would lay the groundwork for the majority's central argument that a section 7 analysis here should involve a "balancing" of interests.

Iacobucci and Arbour found that section 83.28 engages a person's liberty interest, the right to silence, and the right against self-incrimination; but they also found that the provision contains a number of protections against self-incrimination, including "use immunity" (protection from having incriminating testimony used against a person in a later proceeding) and "derivative use immunity" (protection against using incriminating testimony to obtain other evidence).[50] They noted the concern that compelled testimony obtained in this context could be passed on to foreign governments for use in prosecutions abroad; or it could be used against non-citizens in deportation proceedings within Canada.[51] But in response to these concerns, they suggested that, if a person facing deportation or extradition were to raise the issue, section 7 would be engaged and to prevent its being breached, certain orders could be made under section 83.28 to provide for immunity. The scheme itself was therefore consistent with section 7 by virtue of the need to "strike a balance" between "the principle against self-incrimination" and "the state's interest in investigating offences."[52] After stating the need for such a balance, the analysis went no further than the assertion that "[i]n order to meet the s. 7 requirements, the procedural safeguards found in s. 83.28 must necessarily be extended to extradition and deportation proceedings."[53]

Arbour and Iacobucci neglected the more obvious concern that section 7 rights could readily be breached if the immunity provided for in the terms of an order were ignored by a foreign nation to which Canada had extradited or deported a person who had given compelled testimony. In other words, although a judge can order that a person who is compelled to testify be given immunity, he or she might still be deported to a nation that submits them to torture or cruel and unusual punishment. By glossing over this possibility, and asserting a need to balance state and individual interests at the section 7 stage, the Court has once again circumvented the need to consider the possibility that investigative hearings could, in some cases, constitute a violation of section 7, which may or may not then be justified in a section 1 analysis.

Turning then to the question of judicial independence, Iacobucci and Arbour asked whether "a reasonable and informed person would conclude that the court under s. 83.28 is independent."[54] They suggested that the crux of the case against investigative hearings, on grounds of judicial independence, is that the scheme forces the judiciary to play a role traditionally belonging to the executive — partaking, that is, in the investigation and evidence-gathering stage of the criminal process, as opposed to being an independent decision maker at the end of it. They rejected this argument by noting that judges do play a role in proceedings that have an "investigatory purpose," such as wire-tap or search-warrant authorizations, or applications for DNA warrants.[55] The important point is that "[t]he place of the judiciary in such investigative contexts is to act as a check against state excess."[56] In the particular case of investigative hearings, "[t]he function of the judge… is not to act as "an agent of the state," but rather, to protect the integrity of the investigation and, in particular, the interests of the named person vis-àvis the state."[57] This entails ensuring the questioning is "fair and relevant," and making sure terms and conditions are not imposed "in a manner which goes beyond the role of the judiciary as guardian of the Constitution";[58] however, the meaning of this phrase is not entirely clear in the judgment. Finally, the majority concluded, whether the reasonable, informed person would consider that the investigative hearing scheme compromised judicial independence turns largely on the fact of the hearing being held *in camera*.[59] This concern is dealt with by reading the presumption of openness into the scheme, as proposed in *Re: Vancouver Sun*.

By contrast to the views of the majority, the dissenting opinion of Justice LeBel, on behalf of himself and Justice Fish, concluded that the scheme contemplated in section 83.28 compromises judicial independence and is unconstitutional for this reason alone. He arrived at this conclusion in part because he took a stricter view of what it means for the judiciary to be independent, and a more cautious view of the problems that can arise if courts take on the role envisioned in section 83.28.

Justice LeBel's analysis of the concept of judicial independence turns on a distinction he draws between the "individual" and "institutional" dimensions of that independence.[60] The latter requires courts as institutions to function independently from the executive branch not only in a practical sense (administratively and otherwise), but also in terms of appearances.[61] As LeBel writes,

> although they do discuss the institutional dimension of judicial independence, [Justices] Iacobucci and Arbour seem to have inferred the existence of judicial independence from the individual independence of the judge acting pursuant to s. 83.28 without considering whether the institutional dimension was in fact protected. In my colleagues' view, if a judge conducting an investigation pursuant to this provision fails, in exercising his or her discretion, to uphold the rights and freedoms of the person being examined, then, and only then, could it be concluded, after the fact, that judicial independence had been compromised.[62]

Nor could the requirements of "institutional" independence be satisfied by a different judge handling an investigative hearing separate from the trial itself.[63] This is one case, in other words, in which appearances do matter: "without the appearance of a clear separation of powers between the judicial, executive and legislative branches, judicial independence cannot be said to exist."[64]

LeBel was also critical of the role played by judges in an investigative hearing. "Section 83.28... requires judges to preside over police investigations."[65] It would be difficult for a presiding judge to protect the rights of the person examined because of "the overly broad discretionary powers wielded by the judge, the legislative objectives behind the provision and the very nature of these proceedings."[66] It would be difficult to rule on objections — given the amendments to the *Canada Evidence Act* (discussed in the previous chapter); given the fact that rules of evidence in this context are developed for the adjudication of an accused person's culpability; and given the judge's lack of access to "the full record of the police investigation."[67] There would also be a wide discrepancy in the way judges would individually approach their role under the section:

> To my mind, a judge's individual perception of his or her role will necessarily affect the nature and conduct of the examination. Thus, some judges will be more inclined to protect the fundamental rights of the person being examined, while others, who are more conservative, will adopt a contrary approach.[68]

This might be another way of saying that the role of the court envisioned in section 83.28 is not one analogous to any other played by judges in our legal system.

The majority had sought to justify the role of the judge in this context as a protector of the individual against the state, and asserted that the role was therefore analogous to the one judges played elsewhere in the criminal law. LeBel counters this argument by distinguishing what judges do in those other areas of the criminal law. He notes that section 83.28 entails powers distinct from those exercised in wiretap and search-warrant applications because the latter involve "specific investigative techniques": the judge's involvement in the investigation is indirect in those contexts. In other words, it is limited to the granting or refusing of authorization.[69]

In addition, Justice LeBel notes that a reasonable member of the public, looking at the role of the judge in what amounts to an early stage in a police investigation, together with the increased powers given to the state to combat terrorism in recent legislation, would receive the impression of the procedure contemplated in section 83.28 as one in which the judiciary and executive had become "allies."[70] He concluded:

> I believe that s. 83.28 compromises the institutional dimension of judicial independence.... The tension and fears resulting from the rise in terrorist activity do not justify such an alliance. It is important that the criminal law be enforced firmly and that the necessary investigative and punitive measures be taken, but this must be done in accordance with the fundamental values of our political system. The preservation of our courts' institutional independence belongs to those fundamental values.

The suggestion here is that the majority has sought to justify an alliance of the judiciary and the executive in light of concerns about how to best deal with terrorism: thus, on some level the majority's reading of the investigative hearing scheme as constitutional is justified.

Security Certificates in Question

The security certificate regime that was used in *Suresh* has come to play a more important role in the government's dealings with terrorist suspects who are not citizens of Canada. The certificate regime has been a part of immigration law since the late 1970s. It was added to the *Immigration Act* in 1988 in something close to its present form, and was carried over in substantially the same form in the *Immigration and Refugee Protection Act* of 2002.[71] Between 2000 and 2003, the government issued security certificates to arrest five Muslim men believed to be associated with terrorism and has detained them for periods ranging from two to six years, with one detainee at present remaining in custody indefinitely. Separately, the five detainees have brought a number of court challenges to the certificate regime.[72] Many have invoked the detainee's rights under section 7 of the Charter, but in *Re: Charkaoui*[73] the Federal Court of Appeal upheld the constitutionality of the regime and found it consistent with the "principles of fundamental justice." This decision was appealed to the Supreme Court of Canada, in a case that combined the appeals of two other detainees and provided the most significant post-September 11th judicial assessment of the security certificate regime to date. The Court found certain aspects of the regime inconsistent with the principles of fundamental justice: it also found that the resulting breach of section 7 was not justifiable under section 1. But for reasons to be explored below, the Court's proposals for rectifying the breach of section 7 suggest a view of "fundamental justice" that continues to diverge from principles central to the administration of justice.

Briefly, the security certificate regimes works as follows. Section 34 of the *Immigration and Refugee Protection Act* states that a permanent resident or foreign national is "inadmissible" to Canada "on security grounds" for a number of possible reasons, including "engaging in terrorism," or being involved with an organization that is engaged in terrorism, or "being a danger to the security of Canada." Section 77 allows the Minister of Citizenship and Immigration and the Minister of Public Safety and Emergency Preparedness, together, to sign a certificate stating that a permanent resident or foreign national is inadmissible to Canada on grounds of "security" or "serious criminality," among others. Once signed, the certificate functions as a warrant for the person's arrest and detention, pending deportation. A hearing in Federal Court must then be held within forty-eight hours of arrest in the case of a permanent resident, and within 120 days for a foreign national.[74] The Court may conduct the hearing *in camera*; prevent the disclosure of information to the subject of the certificate; consider information or evidence in private (for up to seven days after the matter has been referred for determination); and can hear all or part of the evidence in the absence of the person named in the certificate and their counsel.[75] The Court can receive into evidence "anything that, in the opinion of the judge, is appropriate." The person named in the certificate may receive only a summary of the information or evidence against them sufficient to "enable them to be reasonably informed of the circumstances giving rise to the certificate"; this summary would exclude any information that, if disclosed, would be "injurious to national security."[76] The test on review of the certificate is simply "whether the certificate is reasonable and whether the decision on the application for protection, if any, is lawfully made."[77] If it is found reasonable, deportation proceedings begin.

Among the many concerns raised by critics of the certificate regime, four stand out on a plain reading of the provisions. If a detainee is not shown all of the evidence on which the judge is basing his or her decision, there is a risk that the detainee may fail to speak to a point that he or she might be in a position to address or contradict. The kind of information that might be considered by the judge is so broad in scope that it might be altogether untrustworthy — it may be derived, for example, from torture. Moreover, with the ability to hold hearings *in camera*, and the ability to withhold some of the information from the detainee, the judge loses the benefit of a strong adversarial challenge to the state's case by counsel for the detainee. And finally, if it is decided that a person is to be deported, but he or she faces the risk of torture if deported, the scheme can result (as it has in the case of Hassan Almrei) in an indefinite detention.

The point that seems to have gained most traction among the judiciary is the lack of a meaningful adversary who might challenge the government's case on behalf of the detainee. In a speech to the Canadian Institute for the Administration of Justice Conference, in March of 2002, Justice Hugessen of the Federal Court had this to say about the role of judges in certificate hearings:

> This is not a happy posture for a judge, and you are in fact looking at an unhappy camper when I tell you about this function. Often, when I speak in public I make the customary disavowal that I am not speaking for the Court and I am not speaking for my colleagues but I am speaking only for myself. I make no such disavowal this afternoon. I can tell you because we talked about it, we hate it. We do not like this process of having to sit alone hearing only one party, and looking at the materials produced by only one party. If there is one thing that I learned in my practice at the Bar, and I

have managed to retain it through all these years, it is that good cross-examination requires really careful preparation and a good knowledge of your case. And by definition, judges do not do that, we do not have any knowledge except what is given to us and when it is only given to us by one party we are not well suited to test the materials that are put before us.

We greatly miss, in short, our security blanket which is the adversary system that we were all brought up with and that, as I said at the outset, is for most of us, the real warranty that the outcome of what we do is going to be fair and just. It might be helpful if we created some sort of system somewhat like the public defender system where some lawyers were mandated to have full access to the CSIS files, the underlying files, and to present whatever case they could against the granting of the relief sought.... I am not sure what the judges of the Federal Court are doing in this picture and if I may be forgiven for using the expression, I sometimes feel a little bit like a fig leaf.[78]

The question is whether the effect of introduction of *amicus curiae*, or counsel with special security clearance, to advocate on behalf of the detainee would be to make the certificate regime fairer and more consistent with conventional approaches to adversarial justice.

The Case of Adil Charkaoui

Although Adil Charkaoui is only one of three detainees whose case formed the basis of a challenge to security certificates in the Supreme Court of Canada, a brief review of the facts in his case helps to place the issues in a social and political context. Charkaoui is a French and Arabic speaking Muslim immigrant from Morocco who came to Montreal with his parents in the mid-1990s, when he was in his early twenties. He had travelled throughout the Middle East, North Africa, and Pakistan in the late 1990s for what he claims were employment and family purposes. In the course of these travels, he is alleged to have made the acquaintance of persons involved in radical Muslim terrorist groups active in Spain, Morocco, and Pakistan. Among the evidence that has been disclosed is an identification made by two convicted terrorists presently in custody in the United States. As Federal Court of Appeal Justices Décary and Létourneau noted:

Ahmed Ressam had [recognized Charkaoui] in two photos, adding that he had met him in Afghanistan in the summer of 1998 when the two were training in the same camp. Upon seeing the appellant's photograph, Mr. Ressam identified the appellant under the name of Zubeir Al-Maghrebi, just as Abou Zubaida had done one month previously.[79]

On the basis of this and other, undisclosed information, Charkaoui was arrested in May of 2003 in Montreal and held on a certificate until being released on bail in February of 2005.

At the time of his arrest, Charkaoui was a student at the University of Montreal and ran a pizzeria with his father. He has continuously denied ever being involved with a terrorist organization or in any conspiracy to commit a terrorist act. Upon his release he has continued to pursue his studies and now works in Quebec as a French teacher.[80] The Supreme Court of Canada granted him leave in two further appeals in 2008 — one relating to the destruction of secret evidence in his case by CSIS and the other relating to deportation to torture. (At the time of this writing, the Court has partially allowed the first appeal by confirming the duty to disclose information, subject to being vetted by a judge, but declined to grant a stay of proceedings).

Charkaoui's challenge to the certificate regime involved a number of arguments, in both the Federal Court of Appeal and the Supreme Court of Canada; but for the purposes of this chapter, I focus on those relating only to section 7 of the Charter.[81] At the Court of Appeal, those arguments turned on the question of whether "sections 77 and 78 of the [*Immigration and Refugee Protection Act*] contravene the rights under the Charter with respect to a fair trial before an independent and impartial tribunal, when, for example, the designated judge must determine the "reasonableness" of the security certificate issued by the ministers and not the merits of the case?" Charkaoui had argued that the "cumulative effect" of a number of factors amounted to a breach of "the right to a fair and equitable hearing by an impartial and independent tribunal." Among these factors were the claims that "the decision that leads to his inadmissibility is taken by the executive authority and not by a judge"; "the decision of the designated judge is made on the basis of secret evidence to which the appellant does not have access"; "there is no means for him to test the validity and credibility of this information and thus it is difficult if not impossible for him to refute it'" and

> the standard of evidence adopted by Parliament to justify the issu-
> ance of a security certificate is too minimal, since it is enough to
> have reasonable grounds to believe that the acts described in section
> 34 have occurred, are occurring or may occur when this standard
> should have been more stringent and require that the acts be proved
> according to the standard of the balance of probabilities.[82]

The Court dealt summarily with all of the grounds except the argument that the certificates deprive one of liberty on the basis of secret evidence, less than full disclosure and the appellant's inability to test the credibility of the information at issue. Turning to these, Appeal Justices Décary and Létourneau wrote:

> These three factors are related [and...] are, in fact, at the heart of this particular problem posed by the need to protect national security while respecting the principles of fundamental justice where there is an infringement of someone's right to life or security. They derogate in a significant way from the adversarial process normally adhered to in criminal and civil matters. They raise — properly in this context — the following question: does the special process established by Parliament to determine whether the executive's denial of access to Canada of a permanent resident, his arrest and his detention are justified, comply with the principles of fundamental justice?[83]

The Court concedes that while some evidence may be withheld from the detainee, the evidence against him or her will usually be derived from various sources, and will "either in whole or in the form of a summary... allow him to gain reasonable knowledge of the content, nature and scope of the evidence."[84] And the detainee should console him or herself that "while there is no denying that it is harder... to test the validity and credibility of the information that is not disclosed to him, the fact is that he is assisted in this task by the designated Judge who has the heavy responsibility of maintaining a balance between the parties and accordingly respect for the principles of fundamental justice."[85] They concluded:

> If we were to accept the appellant's position that national security cannot justify any derogations from the rules governing adversarial proceedings we would be reading into the Constitution of Canada an abandonment by the community as a whole of its right to survival in the name of a blind absolutism of the individual rights enshrined in that Constitution....
>
> The individual right to liberty and the security of the person can only be exercised within an institutional framework or social order that commands respect and is respected. It no longer has much meaning or scope when, collectively, the society charged with ensuring its protection has lost its own right to liberty and security as a result of terrorist activities that it was powerless to prevent or eradicate owing to this individual right that it was to protect and intended to protect. The choice, as Justice Jackson said in *Terminiello v. Chicago*... "is not between order and liberty. It is between liberty with order and anarchy without either."[86]

Notably, the derogations from the "rules governing adversarial proceedings" described here are found to be consistent with "fundamental justice." The derogations are not in breach of section 7 but justifiable under section 1. They instead form part of a new reading of "fundamental justice" — one in which Chief Justice Richard of the Federal Court, the third judge in this case, had also concurred.

A unanimous panel of nine justices of the Supreme Court of Canada came to the opposite conclusion. To focus again only on the section 7 argument, Chief Justice McLachlin, writing on behalf of the Court, formulated the question in this way: does the procedure in the Act for determining the reasonableness of the certificate and review of the detention infringe section 7, and, if so, can it be justified under section 1? The Court found that the regime engages section 7 rights because a certificate results in a person's detention and can result in his or her deportation to a country in which his or her safety or liberty is in jeopardy. The procedure for deciding whether a certificate is reasonable and for reviewing the detention was found to be in violation of section 7 because both fail to provide the fair hearing that the "principles of fundamental justice" require.

The Court found that the right to a fair hearing includes the right to a hearing before an independent and impartial judge, as well as the right to know the case against one and the opportunity to answer. In this case, the judge presiding over a certificate hearing maintains independence and impartiality, but because of the provision for the use of secret evidence and *in camera* hearings that exclude the detainee, the right to know the case and to make full answer and defence is violated. There is a real danger, the Court recognized, that a judge could decide matters without all of the information available, precisely for the reason that the detainee was unable to speak to or contradict a point raised by the information kept secret — since she or he was unaware of it. To satisfy the requirements of section 7, "either the person must be given the necessary information, or a substantial substitute for that information must be found."

Notably, the Court sought to return to Justice Lamer's original approach to section 7 interpretation in the *B.C. Motor Vehicle* reference. On that approach, the balancing of state and individual interests should not take place when assessing whether the principles of fundamental justice have been adhered to. As Chief Justice McLachlin wrote,

> while administrative constraints associated with the context of national security may inform the analysis on whether a particular process is fundamentally unfair, security concerns cannot be used to excuse procedures that do not conform to fundamental justice at the s. 7 stage of the analysis. If the context makes it impossible to

adhere to the principles of fundamental justice in their usual form, adequate substitutes may be found. But the principles must be respected to pass the hurdle of s. 7. That is the bottom line.[87]

In this case, the adequate substitute the Court had in mind is the use of "special advocates," or lawyers with security clearances who would be shown the secret evidence and provided an opportunity to cross-examine based on it.

With an acceptable alternative in view, the Court concluded that the certificate regime could not be justified under section 1. Under that section, the Court can decide that a violation of rights is justified if the government has met certain conditions. The first is that the measure or law by which the government seeks to limit rights must have a "pressing and substantial objective." The objective in this case — "the protection of Canada's national security and related intelligence sources"[88] — is pressing and substantial. The state must then establish that the law or measure is proportionate to the objective. A key part of assessing this is to ask whether the law or measure represents a minimal impairment of the right in question. The Court noted that, although "Parliament is not required to use the perfect, or least restrictive, alternative to achieve its objective," the ability to point to the possible use of special advocates suggested that a less restrictive alternative was available. For this reason, the certificate regime could not be justified under section 1.

In light of the general concerns raised about the certificate regime, set out above, the Court's decision in this case leaves a number of issues unresolved. One is whether the addition of special advocates alone would ensure a fair hearing; another is what we can infer about the Court's position on the rest of the certificate regime and whether it is consistent with the principles of fundamental justice.

To address the first question, special advocates alone would arguably not guarantee a fair hearing. The judge could still receive evidence, and hold hearings with respect to it, in the detainee's absence. Disclosure to the detainee would also continue to be as limited as before. Parliament's amendment of the security certificate regime in response to *Charkaoui*, raises precisely these concerns. Commenting on the regime as amended by Bill C-3, Craig Forcese notes:

> A special advocate can never share the secret information with the interested person. Thus, there will never be a case in which that person can inform a special advocate that the government's chief witness (say, a secret detainee interrogated by an allied intelligence agency has a personal animus prompting him to fabricate a story. For this reason, issues of credibility — the meat and potatoes of a fair trial — cannot be effectively raised by advocates. (Forcese 2008)

Forcese also notes that Bill C-3 fails to provide special advocates with a basis on which to "seek and review government records not already disclosed to the court." Advocates must therefore rely on the government's own decisions about what may or may not be relevant. This is a significant concern because, as Forcese writes,

> what the government considers "relevant" and what a special advocate charged with defending the best interest of the detained person considers "relevant" will not always correspond. This discrepancy of views has arisen in Britain, where the government has sometimes failed to give special advocates relevant (and exculpatory) information. It is also an observation affirmed by the Arar commission experiences: Commission counsel (because they were able to compel everything from the government) found information the government initially had declined to disclose. (Forcese 2008)

Forcese also raises the concern that Bill C-3 does not expressly affirm the "ability of the advocate to meet the interested person once the former has seen the secret information." A judge has the discretion to allow this, but as Forcese points out, a similar provision in Britain has resulted in "little or no contact, hurting the advocate's effectiveness" (Forcese 2008).

But apart from the question of whether special advocates make the process more or less fair, the Court's decision in *Charkaoui* can be taken to infer a great deal more about the Court's position on certificates and the "principles of fundamental justice" than is apparent on first reading. If the only aspect of the regime that constitutes a violation of those principles is the inability of the detainee to obtain full disclosure and to respond, then it follows that all of the other concerns raised about the scheme are consistent with fundamental justice, or not inconsistent. In short, these include the ability to arrest, detain, and eventually deport (possibly to torture) a person, on reasonable suspicion, with very limited means of testing the evidence or becoming aware of it in the first place. The evidence itself might be derived from torture by a foreign government. In addition, if a detainee were not to be deported, in order to avoid torture, the regime allows for the administrative limbo of indefinite detention, without charge or conviction. Bill C-3 suggests that all of these questionable aspects are consistent with fundamental justice by dealing only with the concerns raised by the Court in *Charkaoui*. (The bill also includes a provision clarifying that the prohibition in section 269.1 of the *Criminal Code* on the use of evidence obtained by torture or "inhuman or degrading treatment" also applies to security certificate provisions.) In substance, Bill C-3 calls for the use of special advocates, for the provision of regular reviews of a detainee indefinitely detained, and for a speedier initial review following a foreign national's initial arrest. While all of these amendments are laudable, it is still clear that, if the Court had gone further, Parliament would have followed.

Conclusion

In all three cases discussed above, courts are seen to analyze the meaning of "fundamental justice" in section 7 of the Charter by balancing individual and state interests. Rights are curtailed as the challenges facing national security appear to justify new perspectives on what is reasonable. The Supreme Court of Canada's apparent shift in the direction of detainee's rights in *Charkaoui* conceals a deeper consistency with the thrust of its earlier decisions in *Suresh* and *Re: Application under s. 83.28*. In all of these cases, the Court advances a reading of anti-terror measures that contemplate clear departures from the conventional principles of the administration of justice as consistent with section 7. We are left with an emerging jurisprudence that betrays a divide within the judiciary about which departures from convention are thought to be justified, and another divide between the court and its commentators on an idea of "fundamental justice" and a range of practical realities that in fact diverge greatly from it.

Notes

1. *Suresh v. Canada (Minister of Immigration)*, [2002] 1 S.C.R. 3.
2. *Re: Application under s. 83.28 of the Criminal Code*, [2004] 2 S.C.R. 248.
3. *Charkaoui v. Canada (Citizenship and Immigration)*, [2007] 1 S.C.R. 350.
4. Part I of the *Constitution Act, 1982*, being Schedule B to the *Canada Act 1982* (U.K.), 1982, c. 11 [hereinafter, Charter].
5. S.C. 2001, c. 27 [*hereafter, IRPA*].
6. [1985] 2 S.C.R 586.
7. Paragraph 19.
8. [1984] 2 S.C.R. 145.
9. Paragraphs 22 to 26.
10. Paragraph 25.
11. Paragraph 29.
12. Ibid.
13. Paragraphs 73 to 75.
14. Paragraph 85.
15. This case precedes the more elaborate test for a section 1 justification set out in *R. v. Oakes* [1986] 1 S.C.R. 103, but the law in question would probably have failed the proportionality stage of that analysis.
16. *Rodriquez v. British Columbia (Attorney General)*, [1993] 3 S.C.R. 519.
17. In *Suresh*, at paragraph 11, the Court refers to a 2001 report from Amnesty International attesting to the use of torture in Sri Lanka.
18. R.S.C. 1985, c. 1-2.
19. Security Certificates are now issued by the Minister of Citizenship and Immigration and the Minister of Public Safety and Preparedness.

20. See sections 40.1(3) to (11).
21. This is noted at paragraph 13 of the Supreme Court of Canada decision; see also the trial decision at (1999), 173 F.T.R. 1.
22. This decision is summarized at paragraph 14 of *Suresh*.
23. Paragraph 18.
24. Paragraph 16.
25. Ibid.
26. [2000] 2 F.C. 592.
27. At paragraph 42.
28. [2001] 1 S.C.R. 283.
29. Ibid. paragraphs 45 and 47.
30. Specifically, section 25, *Extradition Act*, R.S.C. 1985, c. E-23.
31. Paragraph 38.
32. [1991] 2 S.C.R. 779.
33. [1991] 2 S.C.R. 858.
34. Paragraph 69, *Burns*.
35. From the headnote, *Burns*.
36. Paragraph 133.
37. For a further comparison of *Burns* and *Suresh* on section 7, see Peter Carver (2002: 482-5).
38. Paragraph 49, *Suresh*.
39. Paragraph 58.
40. Paragraph 60.
41. Can. T.S. 1976 No. 47. The other international treaties cited include the *Geneva Convention Relative to the Treatment of Prisoners of War* (1949) Can. T.S. 1965 No. 20; the United Nation's *Universal Declaration of Human Rights* (1948) GA Res. 217 A (III), U.N. Doc. A/810; the *European Convention for the Protection of Human Rights and Fundamental Freedoms* (1950) 213 U.N.T.S. 221, Article 3.
42. Paragraph 74. The cases cited are H.C. 6536/95, *Hat'm Abu Zayda v. Israel General Security Service*, 38 I.L.M. 1471 (1999); *Secretary of State for the Home Department v. Rehman*, [2001] 3 W.L.R. 877.
43. Paragraph 76.
44. Paragraph 78.
45. Bill S-3, 39th Parliament — 2nd Session, 2007.
46. The verdict and a global summary of the case can be found in *R. v. Malik and Bagri*, 2005 BCSC 350.
47. *(Re) Vancouver Sun* [2004] 2 S.C.R. 332.
48. See paragraphs 81 and 170 of the decision.
49. Paragraphs 39 and 40.
50. See paragraphs 71 and 72.
51. Paragraph 74.
52. Paragraph 78.
53. Paragraph 79.
54. Paragraph 83.
55. Paragraph 86.
56. Ibid.
57. Paragraph 87.

58. Paragraph 88.
59. Paragraphs 89 and 90.
60. Paragraph 172.
61. Ibid.
62. Paragraph 177.
63. Paragraph 178.
64. Paragraph 179.
65. Paragraph 180.
66. Ibid.
67. Paragraph 182 and 183.
68. Paragraph 184.
69. Paragraph 188.
70. LeBel J. is borrowing here from language used by David Paciocco (2002: 233), a source cited in the decision at paragraph 186.
71. Kent Roach and Gary Trotter note that as of 2005, Canada had issued twenty-seven security certificates (2005: 967).
72. In addition to Adil Charkaoui, the following have been detained and have launched challenges to various aspects of the security certificate regime: Hassan Almrei, Mohammed Harkat, Mohammad Mahjoub and Mahmoud Jaballah. See, for example, *Almrei v. Canada (Minister of Citizenship and Immigration)* 2005 FCA 54; *Harkat v. Canada (Minister of Citizenship and Immigration)*, [2004] F.C.J. No. 1104; *Canada (Minister of Citizenship and Immigration) v. Mahjoub*, 2004 FC 1028; *Re: Jaballah* 2005 FC 399.
73. *Charkaoui (Re)* 2004 FCA 421, [2005] 2 F.C.R. 299.
74. Section 77, *IRPA*.
75. Section 78(1), *IRPA*.
76. Ibid.
77. Section 80, *IRPA*.
78. This passage is cited in *Harkat v. Canada*, at paragraph 19.
79. *Charkaoui v. Canada* (Citizenship and Immigration) 2004 FCA 421, Section 18.
80. The history and case against him are set out in some detail at the outset of the decision on granting Charkaoui conditional release from custody: *Charkaoui, Re*, 2005 FC 248.
81. *Charkaoui (Re)* 2004 FCA 421, [2005] 2 F.C.R. 299.
82. Paragraph 62, ibid.
83. Paragraph 75, ibid.
84. Paragraph 77, ibid.
85. Paragraph 82, ibid.
86. Paragraph 100, ibid.
87. *Charkaoui v. Canada* (Citizenship and Immigration) [2007] 1 S,C.R. 350.
88. Ibid., paragraph 23.

Chapter 3

Accountability Lost? Law Enforcement in the Age of "National Security"

Long before September 11th, the distinction between law enforcement and intelligence-gathering operations was often blurred. With the inclusion of terrorism offences in the *Criminal Code*, however, the line becomes harder to draw: at that point the Royal Canadian Mounted Police and related law-enforcement agencies began to administer more of Canada's national security mandate. Among the many important issues raised by this shift in responsibility is whether the existing mechanisms for ensuring the accountability of law enforcement provisions are adequate to this broader mandate. The problem of accountability in this context is compounded by two further developments: more work is being done by complex networks of interrelated agencies, both within Canada and abroad; and the government can now insist upon the secrecy of a much broader range of information and activity.

I propose to explore these issues by first addressing why accountability is important to both the rule of law and to the conventional principles that have guided the administration of justice. I then turn to the development and scope of the mandates and accountability mechanisms of the RCMP and the Canadian Security and Intelligence Service (CSIS), before and after 2001. This is followed by a discussion of the events relating to Maher Arar and the Arar Commission, which serve as an object lesson in the challenges of putting the principle of accountability into practice in the national security context, after the enactment of the *Anti-Terrorism Act* (*ATA*). In the final section, I assess the Arar Commission's recommendations for improving the accountability of the RCMP and other state agencies in the national security field. I argue that, although the Commission's proposals might improve upon existing review and oversight mechanisms, these proposals still assume that secrecy should now play a central role not only in the accountability mechanisms of civilian intelligence, but also in those of law enforcement. In adopting this position, the Commission uncritically follows a line of argument that can be traced through recent court decisions endorsing the necessity and validity of greater protection for state secrecy, to Parliament's own justification in 2001 for expanding privilege in the *Canada Evidence Act*. The Arar Commission, the more recent Iacobucci Internal Inquiry[1] and policy statements of the current government suggest that the future of accountability over all state agencies in the national security field will be marked by less transparency and more secrecy. In appearing less transparent, the accountability mechanisms that we employ will significantly affect public confidence in whether law enforcement is in fact accountable, and will in turn compromise the extent to which accountability functions effectively in practice.

Why the Idea of Accountability Is Important

The argument in this chapter begins with the premise that maintaining oversight and accountability of law enforcement and intelligence agencies is fundamental to the rule of law, and by implication, the administration of justice. To understand why this is so, consider first the meaning of "accountability" in this context. The authors of a background paper prepared for the Arar Commission approach the concept of accountability in terms of three basic relationships. They argue that, when we invoke the concept of accountability with respect to a public service entity, we imply that it should be subject to some degree of control by a higher entity or authority; that it should have the duty of explaining itself, or justifying its actions — at least to the controlling entity, but possibly to others; and we also imply that by having another entity provide an impartial assessment, the entity at issue enjoys a more legitimate status than it otherwise might (Commission 2004a: 1–3). How, then, are these meanings connected to the rule of law?

The reader may recall the discussion of A.V. Dicey's interpretation of the rule of law in the introductory chapter. The need for accountability on the part of law enforcement and intelligence can be inferred from the first two of Dicey's three readings. To reiterate, the rule of law is "opposed to the influence of arbitrary power," and excludes "arbitrariness... or wide discretionary authority" (1965: 202). The rule of law for Dicey also meant that everyone is equal under the law and no one is exempt from the duty to obey law. The concern on the part of the citizenry, in a society governed by the rule of law, is that those entrusted with the role of enforcing the law may not obey the law. Without mechanisms for accountability, it would be difficult to know whether those involved in law enforcement and intelligence were conducting themselves in accordance with the law, rather than arbitrarily.

Wesley Pue's definition of the rule of law, also cited in the Introduction, articulates other points implied by Dicey's reading. For Pue, we strive for the equality of all before and under the law by insisting that "[a]ll exercise of governmental power... be accountable, visible, and reviewable by the ordinary courts in the ordinary ways" (2003: 270). Seeing an inherent opposition between accountability and secrecy, Pue asserts that "[p]ower exercised in secret is never accountable." On Pue's reading, accountability is closely connected to the notions of transparency and access. Where accountability is theoretically possible, but practically difficult, it is also theoretically weaker.

With the expansion of state privilege and the efforts of law enforcement and intelligence in national security becoming more complex and interconnected, concerns about state power and secrecy have come to the fore. Assessing the importance of the need to hold police accountable, Commissioner O'Connor of the Arar Commission, wrote:

> In police work in general, and arguably more so in national security police work, the police require considerable powers of intrusion. However, those powers must have limits. Most fundamentally, they must be exercised within the context of the values of our free and democratic society — liberty, the rule of law, the principles of fundamental justice and respect for equality. The police are given powers on the condition that they will exercise those powers within the limits of this context. A basic principle of our system is that public institutions, including the police, must be answerable for acting outside the limits placed on their powers. (2006c: 455)

While we can readily appreciate that accountability is indispensable to our legal and political systems, the question of how to hold people accountable in practice is more challenging. It becomes especially challenging when the state begins to insist that more of police and intelligence activity must be kept confidential, given the nature of counter-terrorism and our international commitments with respect to it.

Before proceeding to explore the problem of accountability further, a distinction should be made clear. Accountability is generally understood to function in two ways: by oversight or by review — terms that are not synonymous in the discussion that follows. A review mechanism, as the Arar Commission defines it, "assesses an organization's activities against standards like lawfulness and/or propriety, and delivers a report of that assessment, with recommendations, to those in government politically responsible for the organization" (2006c: 456). It will often do its work after the fact; it functions at arm's length from the entity in question; and it makes recommendations.

An oversight mechanism, by contrast, works within the entity at issue and is involved in the decisions it is meant to oversee. It attempts to ensure accountability by "setting standards against which the organization's activities are evaluated, pre-approving operations, implementing and enforcing recommendations, and/or imposing discipline." Ideally, state entities that exercise power would be subject to both forms of accountability.

In what follows, we explore the creation and mandates of the RCMP and CSIS, and how their mandate and function has changed after September 11th. We then consider the accountability mechanisms relating to both entities in light of the challenges raised by their expanded functions.

The Origins and Purpose of the RCMP and CSIS

The RCMP was formed in 1873 and originated as a kind of military force with the additional powers of peace officers.[2] The force sent members to the Boer War and to battlefields of World War I, but, in that era, it acted more often in the capacity of a domestic police force. The present mandate of the RCMP is set out in section 18(a) of a substantially updated version of the *Royal Canadian Mounted Police Act* that was passed in 1986. That section makes the force responsible for, among other things, "the preservation of the peace, the prevention of crime and of offences against the laws of Canada." The force has contracted with all provinces and territories, except Quebec and Ontario, to provide police services in accordance with this mandate. The force itself is managed by an RCMP Commissioner, who is accountable to (but not directed by) the Minister of Public Safety and Emergency Preparedness.

Early in its history, the RCMP was involved in some national security matters, such as guarding government buildings in Ottawa and providing security for dignitaries. In the inter-war period, this role expanded to include the gathering of intelligence relating to threats to the security of the nation. During the Cold War era, work on national security included surveillance of foreign intelligence agencies operating in Canada, and persons suspected of espionage. As the contemporary era of terrorism began to take shape, in the late 1960s and early 1970s, the force became more involved with the threat of terrorism on Canadian soil, and took an interest in the Quebec Separatist movement, radical student and labour organizations on the far left, and certain aboriginal groups.

As late as the mid-1960s, there were no formal review mechanisms for the RCMP's security intelligence activities, but public interest in the issue became more prominent. In 1966, a Royal Commission on Security (the "Mackenzie Commission") was established to inquire into the "operations of Canadian security methods and procedures."[3] The Commission recommended the creation of a security intelligence service distinct from the RCMP: the Commission made three arguments in supports of its recommendation.

First, it pointed out that the role of a conventional police force and the task of conducting national security investigations are two disparate and essentially different functions. Second, it noted that the police lack the specialized knowledge and training necessary to conduct security intelligence work effectively. Finally, given the intrusive powers and techniques deployed in the course of security intelligence work, the Commission recommended that the body charged with this mandate should be subject to tighter accountability measures than were in place for the RCMP at that time. The Trudeau government declined to accept these recommendations.

The RCMP's involvement in the October crisis of 1970 proved to be a turning point in an understanding of its functions. In response to terrorists acts of the *Front de libération du Québec*, Trudeau invoked the *War Measures Act*: numerous violations of civil liberties followed from an excessive show of force by police and the military at this time. In the aftermath of these events, the federal government asked the McDonald Commission to make further recommendations for reform of the RCMP's role in national security. Reporting in 1981, the Commission recommended a strict separation of security intelligence work from the RCMP and proposed an independent, civilian security service with various forms of external control.

The government accepted many of the Commission's recommendations. In 1985, Parliament passed the *Canadian Security Intelligence Service Act*,[4] which gave CSIS the mandate to

> collect, by investigation or otherwise, to the extent that it is strictly necessary, and [to] analyse and retain information and intelligence respecting activities that may on reasonable grounds be suspected of constituting threats to the security of Canada and, in relation thereto, shall report to and advise the Government of Canada. (section 12)

The phrase, "threats to the national security of Canada," is defined at length in section 2 of the Act: it includes espionage, "foreign influenced activities," and activities or acts "of serious violence against persons or property for the purpose of achieving a political, religious or ideological object within Canada or a foreign state." The Act contemplates the use of a number of intrusive techniques for the gathering of information, including wiretaps or other interceptions of communication, which require authorization by the courts, but may involve applications made *in camera*.[5]

In addition to this form of judicial review, the Act subjects CSIS to review by an Inspector General, who looks to see if the Service has complied with its own policies, and requires the Inspector General to report to what is now the Minister of Public Safety.[6] A further key source of review in the Act is provided through the creation of the Security Intelligence Review Committee

(SIRC), which is a completely independent and external body, with a broad range of investigative powers over the activities of CSIS (discussed in more detail below).[7]

The same year that the *CSIS Act* was passed, the government also passed the *Security Offences Act*,[8] which addressed the RCMP's responsibilities in the area of national security. Section 6 of the Act gives the force the mandate to investigate matters "constituting a threat to the security of Canada within the meaning of the *Canadian Security Intelligence Service Act.*"[9] The specific role of the force is to perform the "duties that are assigned to police officers" with respect to offences that might pose a threat to national security, or the "apprehension of the commission" of such offences (Arar Commission 2004b: 23). The authors of an Arar Commission background paper note that

> the *Security Offences Act* therefore clarified that, even with the advent of a civilian security intelligence agency, the RCMP would still have significant duties in relation to criminal investigations and the prevention of crime that affected national security. It also established the RCMP, as opposed to municipal or provincial police services, as having primary responsibility in relation to such criminal offences. (2004b: 23)

The scope of RCMP activities, as contemplated in this Act, was broad but generally distinct in its nature and purpose from that of CSIS. Whereas the latter was equipped to conduct sophisticated investigations, it did so only for the purpose of advising the government. Although the methods of the RCMP might have been somewhat less sophisticated and less specialized, its primary purpose was to investigate actual offences and make arrests. The two might work together, but with those different aims in view (2004b: 26).

The overlap between their functions would become greater as a new investigative style began to emerge in the RCMP in the late 1980s. "Intelligence-led policing" took hold as an operational strategy at various levels of the police hierarchy. It encouraged the collection and sharing of information, and the analysis of it, through the use of increasingly sophisticated databases. This was a key aspect of the work done by departments in the RCMP that began to specialize in national security, including the National Security Investigation Directorate (NSID) and the National Security Operations Branch (NSOB) — both of which were established in 1988. In 1991, a Criminal Intelligence Directorate was created to oversee and help coordinate the activities of the various National Security Investigation Sections (NSIS). The RCMP soon had its own complex network of teams and departments focused on national security matters (Arar Commission 2004b: 25–29).

The networking within the force also extended to the relationship between the RCMP and CSIS. Initially, their relationship was addressed in the form of a "Ministerial Directive," and later in a "Memorandum of Understanding" (1986). The memorandum states that each entity would provide assistance to the other for the fulfilment of their respective mandates; each would consult the other in the course of conducting national security investigations; each would carry out the investigations under the guidance and direction of the Solicitor General. The agreement also stipulated that all information provided to one or the other entity would remain confidential and not be used in the course of obtaining warrants or as evidence in court proceedings, without the approval of the other party (Arar Commission 2004b: 29–30).

The National Security Mandate of the RCMP after September 11th

With the advent of the *Anti-Terrorism Act* in the fall of 2001, the scope of the RCMP's national security activities expanded significantly. By including terrorist offences in the *Criminal Code*, Parliament made the RCMP responsible for the investigation and prevention of a range of offences that included conspiracy, attempts to commit terrorism offences, and a host of related activities, such as money laundering, and facilitating, harbouring, or concealing actions that may relate in some way to a terrorist offence.[10] The Act also equipped the RCMP with new powers of investigation, including the "investigative hearings" in section 83.28 and 83.29 of the Code (now lapsed but likely to be re-enacted),[11] which allowed the Attorney General to apply to a judge to compel a person, who was not charged with an offence, to appear before the court and answer questions pertaining to a possible terrorist offence. Another important investigative tool was the provision for obtaining a warrant for electronic surveillance without the normal requirement that other avenues of investigation be exhausted or proven ineffective.[12] The warrant could also be extended for a period of up to three years without the subject of the investigation being aware of it.

In addition to amending the *Criminal Code*, the *Anti-Terrorism Act* amended a host of other legislation that affects the scope of RCMP activities in the field of national security. The *Proceeds of Crime (Money Laundering) Act and Terrorist Financing Act* requires banks and other financial institutions to disclose information to the Financial Transactions and Reports Analysis Centre of Canada (FINTRAC), where there are reasonable grounds to suspect a link to a terrorism offence.[13] Pursuant to amendments made to the *Public Safety Act*,[14] FINTRAC, in turn, is authorized to disclose information to police, where it would assist in the investigation of a terrorism offence (Arar Commission 2004b: 40). As a result of these legislative changes, the authors of a background paper to the Arar Commission point out,

most, if not all, actions which affect the national security of Canada have been criminalized. In consequence, virtually all information and intelligence that CSIS would be interested in is potentially also of interest to the RCMP in connection with its national security crime prevention and law enforcement mandate. (2004b: 41)

Drawing a line between policing and intelligence gathering, therefore, has become almost impossible in practice.

The Practical Workings of the RCMP after September 11th

The RCMP acts under the supervision of an RCMP Commissioner, who is accountable to the Minister of Public Safety and Emergency Preparedness. However, the Minister's oversight of the Commissioner is limited to general statements of policy, under the assumption that, in a developed democracy, a healthy measure of "police independence" from the executive is essential (Arar Commission 2004c). Both the Minister and the RCMP itself have issued directives pertaining to the RCMP's national security work. These notionally guide the actions of the Commissioner, and the numerous Deputy Commissioners in the various regions (Arar Commission 2004b: 44).

National security investigations are carried out in various departments of the RCMP, including the Criminal Intelligence Directorate, and its subbranches, the National Security Investigations Branch (NSIB) and the National Security Operations Branch (NSOB). NSOB is primarily responsible for matters taking place within Canada, while NSIB is focused on matters outside of Canada. But the bulk of the work is undertaken by National Security Investigation Sections, which operate in Montreal, Ottawa, Toronto and Vancouver in the form of Integrated National Security Enforcement Teams (INSETs).[15] Within the cluster of these various teams and departments are groups with such special designations as the "Terrorist and Criminal Extremist Special Projects Group," the "Anti-Terrorist Financial Group," and the "Critical Infrastructure Intelligence Section." The point, in other words, is that the apparatus for dealing with national security within the RCMP has now become exceedingly elaborate and complex, and is only made more so by the degree of integration with outside agencies that is common among all of these subgroups.

Consider, for example, the way that INSETs function. These teams were created after September 11th with a view to coordinating the involvement of, among others, police officers from both the RCMP and various provincial and municipal police forces, members of CSIS, the Canada Border Services Agency, the Coast Guard, Citizen and Immigration Canada, the Canada Revenue Agency, and bodies such as the Financial Transactions and Reports Analysis Centre of Canada (FINTRAC) (Arar Commission 2004b: 50). The INSETs draw upon a wide range of institutional resources shared by various police and state agencies: INSETs are not limited in their purview to national security investigations. They also investigate more conventional criminal offences, including organized crime. Their activities raise questions of jurisdiction and authority, which would have to be sorted out before addressing questions of accountability. As the authors of a background paper for the Arar Commission note,

> Because of their integrated nature, the exact nature of the responsibilities among the various partner agencies involved in INSETs is not always clear. As yet, there are no formal agreements in place among such agencies regarding INSETs generally. Members of other police services who join an INSET are seconded to the INSET and are made Supernumerary Special Constables in the RCMP. There are agreements in place between the RCMP and other police services regarding this status. We have examined one such agreement which provides that the officer from a municipal service shall be supervised by the RCMP, but shall remain under the jurisdiction of the municipal service's disciplinary process as well as the appropriate civilian oversight agency. Pursuant to the agreement, the municipal service agrees to hold harmless and indemnify the RCMP in respect of claims arising from the conduct of the officer. (2004b: 50-1)

Other groups and teams within the RCMP's organizational structure, such as "Integrated Border Enforcement Teams" and "Integrated Immigration Enforcement Teams," function in a similarly expansive fashion with respect to other state agencies: these expanded functions raise similar issues of jurisdiction and responsibility.

Mischief can arise from these integrated dealings in many ways. One example is information sharing — the root cause of Maher Arar's misfortunes. The RCMP shares information about national security internally through a central database dedicated to this area. Information is entered into the Secure Criminal Information System at the discretion of the officer dealing with it. The officer makes a judgment call as to the relevance of the data, but members are encouraged to be inclusive. The information in the database is classed in terms of quality, with categories that range from "reliable" to "believed reliable," to "unknown reliability," and finally to "doubtful reliability." Although the RCMP restricts access to the database to members with special clearance, information can be shared with external agencies, including foreign governments, on a "need to know" basis (Arar Commission 2004b: 56–59).

The sharing of information becomes all the more routine as various inter-agency entities are created with national security as their focus. In addition to INSETs, these entities include the recently created Integrated Threat Assessment Centre, which is operated by CSIS but mandated to assess any information relevant to a possible threat to Canada, and to share that information with any agency or department that may require it, including the Department of Public Safety and Emergency Preparedness, other parts of CSIS, the RCMP, the Department of National Defence, the Department of Foreign Affairs, the Privy Counsel Office, Transport Canada, the Canada Border Services Agency, and another inter-agency entity called the Communications Security Establishment (CSE) (Arar Commission 2004b: 68). The CSE is an entity that operates under the purview of the Minister of Defence and deals primarily with foreign intelligence and activities taking place outside of Canada. It is specifically mandated to provide assistance to both federal law enforcement and security agencies, and is empowered to intercept communications with foreigners that begin or end in Canada. The Department of National Defence also has an Intelligence Division, which contains a National Counter-Intelligence Unit that works with CSIS and the RCMP (Arar Commission 2004b: 68–72).

Accountability Mechanisms of the RCMP and CSIS

There are at present no formal accountability mechanisms to correspond to the RCMP's new, expanded national security mandate. The only formal accountability mechanisms in place are those set out in the 1986 amendments to the *RCMP Act*. They include an RCMP External Review Committee, the Commission for Public Complaints Against the RCMP (CPC), and the Auditor General. The *RCMP Act* also allows the Commissioner of the force or the Solicitor General to appoint a Board of Inquiry to investigate and report on the conduct of the force in a given matter (Arar Commission 2004b: 72–78).

Prior to 1986 amendments to the Act, there was no independent civilian review mechanism of the RCMP. Internal directives set guidelines for handling public complaints in a process that amounted, in essence, to an internal disciplinary review procedure. The 1986 Act created both the CPC and External Review Committee. The External Review Committee functions as an external forum for the appeals of internal disciplinary hearings, while public complaints are heard by an entirely separate external body, the CPC (Arar Commission 2004d: 21–29).

In the normal course of events, complaints made to the CPC are investigated by the force, involve hearings internal to the RCMP, and can result in the imposition of penalties — but not directly by the CPC. The Commission (CPC) lacks the power to subpoena documents, to investigate the RCMP's conduct beyond the scope of the complaint itself, to make a finding that is binding on the force, or to award a remedy to the complainant (Arar Commission 2004e: 21). The authors of an Arar Commission background paper note that the CPC is, in effect, an ombudsman. It has no power to impose a penalty. Only the RCMP Commissioner can do that. Its power is the power of persuasion and the publicity that it can engender to persuade. After a hearing, triggered by a complainant's appeal, the Commission issues an interim report, to which the RCMP Commissioner must respond and in which the Commissioner can accept or reject the Commission's findings. The Commission then sends its final report with the Commissioner's response to the minister. The Commission gives its report whatever publicity it thinks would help its position. It notes on its web site that over 94% of the Commission's adverse findings and recommendations are accepted by the RCMP Commissioner. (2004d: 29–30)

The Commission for Public Complaints does, however, have the mandate to initiate an investigation and hold a hearing when it believes it would be in the public interest to do so. An investigation of this kind was undertaken in both the Arar case and in the matter of police conduct at the APEC meeting in Vancouver in 1997. The APEC hearing was the last the Commission has conducted (having conducted a total of only eighteen since the inception of the Commission in 1988) (Arar Commission 2004d: 24). The Commission's investigation into the Arar matter was adjourned pending the outcome of the Inquiry.

By contrast to the CPC, the equivalent body that oversees the conduct of CSIS — the Security Intelligence Review Committee (SIRC) — has a greater ambit of review and more power at its disposal in the course of investigations.[16] The SIRC is entitled to disclosure of information on any of CSIS's activities (including warrants and affidavits used) and ministerial directives. For activities not already drawn to the attention of the SIRC, the CSIS has a duty to report on its conduct to the SIRC (Arar Commission 2004f: 32). The SIRC can summon witnesses and order the production of documents. Like the CPC, however, SIRC's power to "censure" is limited to making recommendations and tabling reports: it can make recommendations to the Director of CSIS, and it reports annually to the Minister, who in turn reports to Parliament.

In a 2002 speech to the Canadian Institute of the Administration of Justice, then Commissioner of the CPC, Shirley Heafey, commented on the disparity of investigative powers between the CPC and those of the SIRC by stating that

> problems are generally drawn to my attention by a complainant. But what happens when a potential complainant doesn't know of the CPC's existence or, worse, is afraid to complain about the actions of the police?… Without a complaint and without the power to randomly review files, it is difficult to investigate and to assess

RCMP use of the new powers.... A search is authorized by warrant issued by a judicial official who has read an affidavit in support of the request for the warrant. If I don't have access to those documents, how can I, in good conscience, assure the Minister of Justice and the Solicitor General that I am overseeing the RCMP's use of these new powers? (cited by the Arar Commission 2004d: 32)

She concluded that the Commission for Public Complaints "requires additional powers and additional resources to restore balance — to balance the new powers and resources given to the RCMP for the purpose of combating terrorism" (Arar Commission 2004d: 32).

The question for both the SIRC and those exercising oversight over the RCMP, is whether either scheme is adequately suited to deal with the kinds of problems encountered in the Arar incident and its aftermath.

The Arar Incident, the Inquiry, and the Cloud of Secrecy

Briefly, Arar's ordeal began in September of 2002 when he was stopped in New York on a return trip from Tunisia with his family. Acting on information obtained by CSIS and passed to American border authorities by the RCMP, Arar was detained for two weeks and then deported to Jordan.[17] In Jordan, Arar was beaten and tortured, and then taken to Syria to a prison where he was tortured further and forced to sign a confession to the effect that he had travelled to Afghanistan and was involved in military training. He was held for over a year.

In the first of two final reports tabled in September of 2006, the Arar Commission found that

> both before and after Mr. Arar's detention in the U.S. the RCMP provided American authorities with information about Mr. Arar which was inaccurate, portrayed him in an unfair fashion and overstated his importance to the investigation. Some of this inaccurate information had the potential to create serious consequences for Mr. Arar in light of American attitudes and practices at the time.[18]

The Commission also found that the information was provided by the RCMP to American authorities without the caveats about sharing information required by RCMP policy. Communications by the RCMP to U.S. Customs destined for inclusion in its enforcement database described Arar and his wife as "Islamic Extremist individuals suspected of being linked to the al Qaeda terrorist movement" (Arar Commission 2006a: 13). The Commission also found that CSIS did not share information with U.S. officials before Arar was detained and deported to Syria, and that neither CSIS nor the RCMP had any part to play in the decision to detain and deport Arar.

Only days after Arar was taken overseas, Canada's then Ambassador to Syria, Franco Pillarella, met with Syrian military officials who agreed to pass on to Canada any information obtained in the course of interrogations. A summary of Arar's confessions was then provided to CSIS and the RCMP. The Commission found that while Arar was detained in Syria, "Canadian agencies relied on information about Mr. Arar received from the Syrians which was likely the product of torture. No adequate reliability assessment was done to determine whether the information resulted from torture" (2006a: 15). The Arar Commission determined that in January of 2003, a few months into Arar's imprisonment in Syria, the RCMP,

> acting through the Canadian Ambassador, sent the [Syrian Military Intelligence] questions for Abdullah Almalki, the subject of the relevant investigation and also in Syrian custody. This action very likely sent a signal to Syrian authorities that the RCMP approved of the imprisonment and interrogation of Mr. Almalki and created a risk that the [Syrian Military Intelligence] would conclude that Mr. Arar, a person who had some association with M. Almalki, was considered a serious terrorist threat by the RCMP. (2006a: 15)

As the months passed, the government resisted calls on the part of Arar's wife, Monia Mazigh, to investigate his whereabouts and the role of state agencies in his deportation. Mazigh was told by authorities that there was no clear consensus in the Canadian government on whether Arar's release should be sought. In retrospect, the equivocation on the part of the government was one of the main reasons Arar's ordeal lasted as long as it did. Three other Muslim Canadian men, Ahmad Abou El-Maati, Abdullah Almalki, and Muayyed Nureddin, were investigated in Canada by the RCMP and CSIS during roughly the same period of time and were all detained in 2002 by Syrian officials when travelling through that country on family visits. They were eventually tortured and imprisoned there as well.[19]

The broader issues raised by these events include the concern that the Canadian government never in fact had credible evidence linking any of these men to terrorism; that the RCMP's actions readily resulted in the decision, even if unintended, to detain Arar in New York and deport him to Syria; that Canadian officials were aware that Arar was being tortured, but ignored the fact; that Canadian officials were potentially the source of information used during Arar's interrogation in Syria; and that, given the allegations of the three other Muslim Canadians detained in Syria at this time, these events might be part of a pattern of such conduct on the part of Canadian authorities.

Before turning in more detail to the work of the Arar Commission, it is important to note what degree of accountability was provided by the existing

RCMP and CSIS oversight and review mechanisms. There were three investigations (Arar Commission 2006b: 541–51). The RCMP's Chief Superintendent Dan Killam conducted an "operational review" into the investigation project that related to Arar. The force also conducted an internal investigation pursuant to the *RCMP Act*. The third investigation, on CSIS's role in the incident, was undertaken by the SIRC.

The RCMP's two internal investigations related to complaints brought by Shirley Heafey of the CPC and the Canadian Civil Liberties Association. Their complaints alleged, among other points, that information about Arar was obtained without following appropriate criteria; that it was divulged to U.S. authorities improperly; and that, once it was divulged and the train of events was set in motion, the RCMP either did not do enough to assist Mr. Arar or actively and wrongfully facilitated his deportation and torture. At the risk of blurring the discrete findings of these investigations, the result might be generally summarized in terms of a small number of concessions: that more information should have been obtained about Arar before deciding he was a "person of interest"; that caveats on the use of information should have been sought before sharing it; and that there was a significant lack of oversight about information sharing among CSIS, the RCMP, and U.S. officials. The effect of these investigations, however, was somewhat muted, due to the fact that the Arar Commission was pending.

By contrast, SIRC's investigation into CSIS's involvement in the Arar incident appears to have been more effective (Arar Commission 2006b: 549–50). After an extensive review of documents from dating from 1993 to 2002, the SIRC found that CSIS had no prior knowledge of the intent on the part of U.S. officials to detain and deport Arar, and had never approved of the RCMP's disclosure of information about Arar to any third party. The SIRC also found that CSIS learned of Arar's detention only on October 2, 2002: soon after CSIS sought information about Arar from Washington. CSIS was also asked by Syrian military intelligence to go to Syria to review information obtained from Arar: the SIRC noted that, since CSIS had no policy on the use of torture, this was not an issue. One of the SIRC's key findings was that its mandate as a review entity prevented it from determining the extent of the RCMP role in the events: this demonstrated a severe limitation in its ability to determine accountability (Arar Commission 2006b: 549). The SIRC recommended that CSIS policy be amended to include a requirement for protection against third-party disclosure in information sharing with the RCMP; that a country's human rights record be considered when deciding whether to travel to that destination; and that sensitive requests, like the one made to Washington, be made a priority. In submissions to the Arar Commission, counsel for the government stated that CSIS's operational policy had been amended in conformity with a number of the SIRC's recommendations, including the first two noted here (Arar Commission 2006b: 549).

The Arar Commission was created in part to assess accountability issues in the field of national security that the earlier reviews by the RCMP and the SIRC were poorly equipped to address. The mandate of the Commission was therefore twofold: to make findings of fact with respect to the Arar incident, and to make recommendations for an accountability mechanism for the RCMP's national security activities. In the course of the Commission's inquiry, however, accountability itself became a central issue precisely by virtue of the government's insistence that so much of the evidence be kept secret. The Committee of Organizations with Intervenor Status at the Arar Commission put the problem in these terms:

> Much of what was supposed to be a public inquiry has been held behind closed doors — only five days of contextual public hearings were held before the inquiry disappeared into eight months of in-camera hearings which excluded Maher's lawyers and organizations that were granted Intervenor Status. The Commission had hoped to issue public summaries of the secret hearings, but the government used the threat of lengthy federal court battles to block their release. The government claimed that releasing this information would threaten national security, but the Commissioner's ruling disagreed, noting that much of what the government suppressed has already been published in the media, or is favourable to Maher. Without access to the evidence presented in these secret hearings, Maher's team and intervening organizations have learned very little on which to base their participation at the inquiry.[20]

After the lengthy period of *in camera* hearings, the Commission resumed hearing evidence for a number of weeks in May and June of 2005. Therefore, the majority of the evidence was heard *in camera*.

The Arar Commission tabled two final reports, one made public in September of 2006 relating to the events in question (2006a, 2006b) and another published in December of 2006 proposing a new review mechanism for the RCMP's national security activities (2006c). Commissioner O'Connor explained at the outset of the first of these reports:

> There are two versions of this Report. One, which may not be disclosed publicly, is a summary of all of the evidence, including that which is subject to national security confidentiality. The public version that you are reading does not include those parts of the evidence that, in the Commissioner's opinion, may not be disclosed publicly for reasons of national security confidentiality.
>
> A good deal of evidence in the Inquiry was heard in closed, or

in camera, hearings, but a significant amount of this *in camera* evidence can be discussed publicly without compromising national security confidentiality. For that reason, this Report contains a more extensive summary of the evidence than might have been the case in a public inquiry in which all of the hearings were open to the public and all transcripts of evidence are readily available. While some evidence has been left out to protect national security and international relations interests, the Commissioner is satisfied that this edited account does not omit any essential details and provides a sound basis for understanding what happened to Mr. Arar, as far as can be known from official Canadian sources.

Finally, it should be noted that there are portions of this public version that have been redacted on the basis of an assertion of national security confidentiality by the Government that the Commissioner does not accept. This dispute will be finally resolved after the release of this public version. Some or all of this redacted information may be publicly disclosed in the future after the final resolution of the dispute between the Government and the Commission. (Arar Commission 2006a: 11–12)

The result, then, is a curious multiplication of narratives. First, there is the full version, then the edited version (for public consumption), and finally, the edited-edited version (for public consumption as approved by the censors). What remains unclear, however, is whether the version with which the Commissioner is "satisfied" — the one that "does not omit any essential details" — is the one that "we are reading," or the one Commissioner O'Connor wanted to publish before the censors had their way.

To put this into context, the government's claim for confidentiality resulted in some fifteen-hundred words of the first report being blacked-out, pursuant to a process set out in section 38 of the *Canada Evidence Act*. The censored portions consisted of words or phrases on certain pages, but in some cases entire paragraphs. A significant portion of the censored text appears in an appendix dealing with Commissioner O'Connor's rulings on an application by the government to keep information confidential relating to CSIS investigations and information-sharing practices. Much of the Commissioner's summary of the application itself is censored, in addition to the Commissioner's proposed summary of the hearing itself (Arar Commission 2006a: 727–45).

Both Maher Arar and the Commission sought disclosure of the redacted material in Federal Court, which ruled on the issue in July of 2006.[21] The question for Justice Noel in that hearing was framed by sections 38.04 and 38.06 of the *Canada Evidence Act*, which consider whether the public interest in disclosure of the material outweighs in importance the public interest in non-disclosure. He found that the public interest in disclosure prevailed with respect to much of the information at issue; but there remained a portion that would be injurious to public interest to disclose, and this has been kept confidential. The Commission's counsel, Paul Cavalluzzo, stated in a press release following the decision that "some important information relating to human rights and torture issues will now be disclosed to the public. As a result, there is more transparency in the process which will lead to more accountability for government officials" (Arar Commission 2007). But what remains unclear is whether the final version, with the addenda, includes all the "essential details" that Commissioner O'Connor wanted to convey.

Assuming it does, both the Arar incident and the Arar Commission of Inquiry still raise a number of concerns about the limits of accountability for law enforcement and intelligence in national security endeavours. Much of the evidence in the Inquiry, and some of the final report intended for the public, remains confidential, even after the Commission determined that it should be disclosed. The suggestion here is that the remaining censored material is negligible and that, in all likelihood, we have all the information we need to be sure that the matter has been adequately reviewed. The problem with this approach, however, is that it results not only in a loss of transparency, but also in the loss of another essential element in the principle of accountability: the confidence of the public that the actors in question are actually being held accountable. In other words, by substituting the performance or spectacle of open hearings, and public examinations of witnesses, with a censored summary of this, the public never in fact sees accountability taking place. The public's confidence that actors are held accountable may not require, in every case, that a pubic hearing be held, but where this is foregone in a favour of a censored summary, it leaves more room for doubt and uncertainty.

It is also important to note that it was always open to the government to issue the final trump card of a "secrecy certificate" (section 38.13 of the *Canada Evidence Act*), which would effectively supersede both the Commission and the Federal Court's opinions about what should be disclosed. This does not so much suggest that a state entity was being held accountable by an independent Commission; rather, it appears to indicate that a state entity was enjoying the protection of the government — as far as it was prepared to extend it. There was a lingering sense, in other words, of lost transparency: one was left with the impression that the state was arbitrarily exercising its power to operate with more or less secrecy.

Can a Solution Be Found in the Models Proposed?

The second part of the Arar Commission's mandate was to "make recommendations for an independent, arm's length review mechanism with respect to the RCMP's national security activities" (Arar Commission 2006c: 17). The Commission set out three specific objectives of its review:

1) to provide assurance that RCMP activities are in conformity with the *Canadian Charter of Rights and Freedoms*, the law and the standards of propriety that are accepted in Canadian society;
2) to foster accountability of the RCMP to government; and
3) to foster accountability to the public, thereby maintaining and enhancing public trust and confidence in the RCMP. (2006c: 456)

The Commission also asked what kind of accountability mechanism was more appropriate for the RCMP in this context: review or oversight? An oversight mechanism was considered to be inappropriate because it would offend the principle of police independence, it would confuse the roles of government and police, and it might also become "implicated in decisions that should be subject to independent review after the fact" (2006c: 457).

In the course of its assessment, the Commission considered the merits of the accountability mechanisms currently in place and found that

> existing accountability and review mechanisms for the RCMP's national security activities are not adequate in large part because of the evolution and increased importance of that national security role. Among the more significant changes have been enhanced information sharing, new legal powers and responsibilities, and increased integration in national security policing. I have also been influenced by the Canadian and international experience with both policing and security intelligence review, and the inability of a complaint-based approach to provide a firm foundation for ensuring that the often secret national security activities respect the law and rights and freedoms. Finally, I conclude that the difficulties that the CPC has encountered in obtaining access to information from the RCMP can undermine the effectiveness of its review function and public confidence in the effectiveness of the review. (2006c: 18)

On this basis, the Commission recommended a new review agency for the RCMP called the Independent Complaints and National Security Review Agency (ICRA), which would be situated within the Commission for Public Complaints after that body had been restructured in various ways. The

ICRA would have a number of enhanced powers relative to the CPC and the SIRC.

The ICRA would investigate and report on complaints made by civilians or third parties. The threshold for deciding whether to proceed with a complaint would be low (given the secrecy surrounding much of the activity at issue and the likelihood that complainants may not have much evidence to present). The ICRA would also have the power to conduct self-initiated reviews. The scope of review would be quite broad: anything relating to the compliance of the RCMP's national security activities with law, policy, ministerial directives or international obligations (Arar Commission 2006c: 18). The Agency would have "extensive investigative powers," similar in nature to those under the *Inquiries Act*,[22] including the power to subpoena witnesses that could include civilians or members of the RCMP or related agencies, and it could also compel disclosure of documents. Its mandate would be to

> conduct self-initiated reviews to ensure that the RCMP's national security activities fall within its law enforcement mandate; that its information sharing practices are appropriate and conform to policy; that its relationships with other domestic and foreign agencies are properly regulated; that its national security investigators are properly trained and show proper respect for human rights and individual liberties; that its communications with foreign countries, including communications when Canadians are being detained abroad, are appropriate; and also to ensure that there is effective review of any operational activities of the RCMP that are integrated with those of other agencies. (Arar Commission 2006c: 20)

The Commission also recommended that the national security activities of five entities, with which the RCMP has been working closely, should also become subject to independent review. In particular, the Commission suggested that the ICRA would be best suited to reviewing integrated activities of the RCMP and the Canada Border Services Agency, while the SIRC should have jurisdiction to review Citizenship and Immigration Canada, Transport Canada, and the Financial Transactions and Reports Analysis Centre of Canada as well as Foreign Affairs and International Trade Canada.

To ensure an "integrated review of integrated national security activities" among the three review agencies — the ICRA, the Communications Security Establishment (CSE) Commissioner and the SIRC — the Arar Commission recommended the creation of an additional entity, the Integrated National Security Review Coordinating Committee (INSRCC). Although its creation would require legislative amendments to allow for information exchange, complaint referrals and joint investigations and reports, it would result in an apparatus for coordinated efforts that is common among analogous agencies in other countries. The Committee would be chaired by members of the three other review bodies, but would not conduct reviews itself. Its mandate would be to "ensure that the statutory gateways are functioning as intended, provide a unified intake mechanism for complaints regarding national security activities of federal entities, and report to the federal government on accountability issues relating to Canada's national security practices and trends, including the effects of those practices and trends on human rights and freedoms" (Arar Commission 2006c: 22).

The Arar Commission's Recommendations and the Limits of Accountability after the Anti-Terrorism Act

Initially tabled in December of 2006, the Commission's second report, and its many recommendations, have yet to be formally adopted by Parliament. However, committees of the House of Commons and Senate, reporting on their (delayed) three-year reviews of the *Anti-Terrorism Act*, did give their approval to a number of the Commission's recommendations. In the summer of 2007, the government of Canada indicated that it would "propose an approach to national security review that will meet the basic objectives set out in the second report of the Commission of Inquiry into the Actions of Canadian Officials in Relation to Maher Arar and is considering options for an enhanced role for Parliamentarians as a key part of these proposals for an improved national security review framework" (Canada, Department of Justice 2007: 25).

The Commission's recommendations would clearly amount to an improvement on existing accountability mechanisms. But whether the coordinated efforts and expanded jurisdiction of the review mechanisms proposed in its report are adequate to address the coordinated efforts of numerous entities working on national security files is questionable. At the very least, the practical and jurisdictional complexities of coordinated national security activities will always pose a challenge for those involved in reviewing them.

The more crucial point here is not that the Commission's proposals for making the RCMP and its partner agencies more accountable may somehow fail in practice; rather, it indicates that the new review models contemplated by the Commission already assume significant departures from the way that accountability is understood by Pue (2003) or implied by Dicey (1965). The Commission departs from that understanding by adopting a line of reasoning that can be traced to Parliament's justification in 2001 for expanding the scope of state secrecy in the *Canada Evidence Act*, and to the courts in *Charkaoui* and *Khawaja*. The argument uncritically adopted here is that secrecy and confidentiality must now play a central role in all matters relating to counterterrorism, including review and oversight. Thus, recommendation 5 of the second report of the Arar Commission states that the ICRA complaints process should include

> (g) open and transparent hearings of a complaint, to the extent possible, but authority for ICRA to conduct all or part of a hearing in private when it deems it necessary to protect national security confidentiality, ongoing police investigations or the identity and safety of sources; and
>
> (h) for purposes of hearings of complaints, discretion by ICRA to appoint security-cleared counsel independent of the RCMP and the government to test the need for confidentiality in regard to certain information and to test the information that may not be disclosed to the complainant or the public; (2006c: 605)

The thrust of these proposals is that confidential hearings and special advocates are less preferable to the ideal course of open hearings, with adversarial justice. But the implication is clear: a large part of these reviews may have to be conducted *in camera*, with *ex parte* hearings (hearings in which only one party appears). The practice of review exemplified by the Arar Commission itself, and the Iacobucci Internal Inquiry (dealing with the three other Canadian detainees relating to the Arar incident), confirms this. Both inquiries have involved numerous *in camera* hearings and evidence often tested not by affected parties but by special advocates. In both cases, the less preferable practices became commonplace.

To understand the logic that the Commission has uncritically adopted here, we need to trace its antecedents. These extend at least as far back as Parliament's assertion in 2001 of the need to expand the scope of state secrecy in the *Canada Evidence Act*. The justification for that change in the law can be gleaned from a policy statement published by the present government in 2007. Issued in response to a recent review of the *Anti-Terrorism Act* by a Commons subcommittee, the statement notes:

> Canada is only in a position to provide the necessary guarantees to another state that information will not be disclosed if the ultimate decision is vested in the Attorney General of Canada and not the courts. In recent litigation concerning section 38 of the [*Canada Evidence Act*], the federal Crown made the following argument:
>
> The consequences of a breach of the third party rule would be significant to Canada, given that it is generally a net importer of sensitive information. While other states may still be willing to share information with Canada, their calculations of risk and benefit might well be different in many cases if they considered as

> potentially unreliable Canada's ability to guarantee the protection of information that was given to it in confidence. This would, in turn, impair Canada's ability to combat terrorism. (Canada, Department of Justice 2007: 16)

On the basis of this logic, the government in 2001 assumed it was justified in broadening the scope of privilege over any "sensitive information" relating to national security that is "of a type that the Government of Canada is taking measures to safeguard" (section 38.01, *Canada Evidence Act*). To ensure that it would have the last word on the matter, the government gave itself the power to issue a certificate that would assert a sweeping form of privilege — a privilege that is subject to judicial review of a very limited sort. The government at that stage would have to show only that the information at issue relates to national defence or security in order to assure its secrecy (section 38.131).

The belief in the need for greater secrecy in any area relating to national security was soon adopted by the courts. In *Charkaoui*, the Supreme Court of Canada found much of the security certificate regime, which works in tandem with the secrecy provisions in the *Canada Evidence Act*, to be consistent with the Charter. The parts of the regime that were most problematic for the Court were those that denied disclosure to the detainee and allowed for *ex parte* hearings on confidential material. The Court found a satisfactory solution in the SIRC's long-standing use of "special advocates," recommending that special advocates might also work well in the context of security certificate proceedings. The prudence of drawing an analogy between a SIRC hearing and a security certificate hearing was never questioned. When, soon after, in *Khawaja*, the Federal Court was asked to assess the validity of *ex parte, in camera* hearings in section 38 of the *Canada Evidence Act*, it followed the Supreme Court's lead. These hearings can be justified to a large extent, the court found, because they allow for the use of special advocates, as now broadly sanctioned in *Charkaoui*. Again, the question was never asked whether an approach that originated with the SIRC — and entails a serious compromise of adversarial justice in that context — was a suitable substitute for adversarial justice in a criminal, rather than an intelligence, case.

The Arar Commission makes the same leap in logic. Where *in camera* hearings have always been appropriate for the SIRC in its review of a secret intelligence agency, they are now assumed to be necessary and appropriate to the review of law enforcement. Where any procedural issues are said to arise in the course of *ex parte* hearings or applications before the proposed ICRA, the use of special advocates is assumed to be an adequate solution. As a consequence, the Commission proposes an accountability mechanism that allows for a great deal of secrecy within its own procedures; moreover, these would also be subject to an additional and entirely separate *Canada Evidence Act* proceeding if the government were to second-guess the decisions of the ICRA and take matters to Federal Court (which the government did in the Arar Commission itself).

Among the most notable aspects of the Commission's recommendations, therefore, is the tendency to internalize the need for secrecy. The latter is now seen to be an essential part of the way review and oversight will function in the counter-terrorism field. Although transparency, openness, and full disclosure are important elements of accountability, they must now be balanced with the need to protect national secrets. There is almost no consideration in the second report of the Arar Commission as to whether the concept of accountability can be sustained in a model that allows for so much secrecy. Commissioner O'Connor does recognize, however, that a trade-off is taking place:

> It is thus essential that the design of a review mechanism for the RCMP's national security activities take account of the fact that a great deal of what needs to be reviewed may not be disclosed publicly. The significant challenge is therefore to come up with a process that, while not fully transparent, still engenders public confidence and trust. (Arar Commission 2006c: 428)

But he insists repeatedly on the need for secrecy and assumes that it is justified to use secrecy in the context of a law enforcement review because it was used in the review of intelligence:

> In my view, a review mechanism requires access to all relevant information necessary to carry out its function effectively. Therefore, with limited and isolated exceptions, the review mechanism should not be barred from information because that information is secret or sensitive. In turn, the review mechanism must itself be subject to obligations not to disclose. As discussed... this approach to review has worked well with CSIS and SIRC, as well as with the Communications Security Establishment (CSE) and the CSE Commissioner. (2006c: 476)

The point that is glossed over here is that each of these contexts is quite distinct. Following Parliament and the courts, the Commission is suggesting, in essence, that if it is acceptable to use secrecy in the review of national security intelligence, it is therefore acceptable to use it in national security matters generally.

The flaw in this argument is that it treats the kind of power exercised by intelligence agencies, such as CSIS or the CSE, as equivalent to the kind of power exercised by the police and other law enforcement agencies. In other words, it might be necessary to conduct reviews of intelligence agencies behind a veil of secrecy, and accept that the extent of "review" and accountability in these contexts will be limited to tabling a confidential report to the executive. The limitation seemed reasonable at one point because the power exercised by those agencies was also limited to gathering intelligence and running surveillance. This was precisely the point of the McDonald Commission and its recommendation to assert a more strict separation of law enforcement and intelligence. Intelligence agencies would necessarily do much of their work in secret, but their power to do mischief would, in theory, be diminished. By contrast, the Arar Commission is proposing that the review of police powers should now be limited in the same ways that we limit the review of intelligence — by doing much of it in secret and trusting quasi-judicial figures or politicians to tell us that it has been done. It is also proposing that we should accept these limits despite the fact that, in the case of law enforcement, the potential for mischief is far greater. As Commissioner O'Connor put it, "In police work in general, and arguably more so in national security police work, the police require considerable powers of intrusion" (2006c: 455). The distinct roles of the RCMP and CSIS in the Arar incident are a good example.

One might argue in response that if less transparency is necessary in the field of national security, this does not necessarily result in a lack of accountability. There is, however, a clear difference between a review exercise that is mostly or entirely confidential and one in which the review is conducted and concluded in public. The one serves the goal of accountability, the other essentially stages it. By virtue of this, we might also say, recalling Pue (2003) and Dicey (1965), that a system or entity that is not seen by the public to be accountable is not one that functions with accountability either. In other words, the public's confidence that entities are being held accountable is an integral part of what it means to have accountability.

The trend that is emerging is to have more secrecy and less transparency. As the justification for the *Canada Evidence Act* amendments becomes more widely accepted, we are likely to see more accountability exercises in the national security context unfolding as the Arar Commission did — involving hearings mostly *in camera*; a lengthy, convoluted dispute with the government over disclosure; followed finally by assurances from the review entity that what was disclosed to the public conveyed the "essential details." When review bodies eventually decide to forego the dispute with government over disclosure, it will not be due to a lack of concern for greater disclosure, but instead due to the fact that the lessons of the Arar Commission will finally have been learned.

The Iacobucci Internal Inquiry is instructive in this respect. It was intended as a kind of extension to the Arar Commission, to deal with the role of CSIS and the RCMP in the detention and torture abroad of three other Canadians. As Toronto journalist Thomas Walkham put it, to call the Inquiry secretive "would be an understatement.... [The] inquiry is so secretive that it censors even the complaints about its obsessive secrecy" (Walkham 2007). The Inquiry's rules of procedure state that "the Inquiry, including the review of documents and the taking of oral evidence, shall be conducted in private, except where the Commissioner is satisfied that it is essential to ensure the effective conduct of the Inquiry that specific portions of the Inquiry be conducted in public" (Walkham 2007). Walkham notes that from the outset "the inquiry's doors have been shut so tight that the credibility of the inquiry — its entire raison d'être — is in doubt. No one expected the government to share its national security secrets with the public. But this inquiry has shared virtually nothing." In the fall of 2007, the three men at the centre of the Inquiry complained of having received almost no disclosure. As Walkham explains, the three men

> have not been given any documents, even non-secret ones. They have not been allowed to cross-examine witnesses. They don't even have a witness list.
>
> There have been no public hearings. Nor have summaries of evidence been provided.
>
> The very fact that the three men complained to the commission about its secrecy was kept secret until Friday. The complainants themselves weren't allowed to talk about it.
>
> And when it did make the complaint public, the commission censored portions — not because they dealt with matters of national security but because they spoke to how the commission was handling its business. (Walkham 2007)

Walkham also raises the critical point that when Justice Iacobucci tables his final report, "no matter how balanced and judicious his findings, he runs the risk that he won't be believed." Taken to its extreme, a review conducted in secret is no longer credibly associated with accountability.

The legacy of the Arar and Iacobucci inquiries may well have as much to do with form as with content. They were meant to ensure that a thorough inquiry was conducted into matters of public concern. The findings made public in both inquires were meant to convey everything worth conveying. Both inquiries were also meant in some way to build confidence in the rule of law, and the administration of justice, by suggesting that the lessons learned would help make law enforcement more accountable in the future. But the impression made by hearings that took place mostly in secret, and final reports that became the objects of contentious debates over secrecy, undermines all of these objectives.

Soon, as result, the practice of accountability in the field of national security may become so disconnected from the notion of transparency, and so ineffective at instilling confidence in the public, that law enforcement will no longer be assumed to be subject to the rule of law in this area. In accepting the belief that more secrecy is needed in all aspects of national security, including accountability, we run the risk of cultivating an indifference on the part of the public as to what goes on behind closed doors. The fate of our legal and democratic systems lies in the balance.

Notes

1. Its full title is the "Internal inquiry into the Actions of Canadian Officials in Relation to Abdullah Almalki, Ahmad Abou El-Maati and Muayyed Nureddin." Inquiry documentation is available at <http://www.iacobucciinquiry.ca/en/home.htm> (last accessed February 8, 2008).
2. I have derived the following history of the RCMP, and details about its mandate and previous operations, from an Arar Commission background paper on the RCMP and national security (2004b).
3. *Report of the Royal Commission on Security* (Mackenzie Report), Minister of Supply and Services Canada, 1969; cited by the Arar Commission (2004b: 10).
4. R.S.C. 1985 c. C-23. (*CSIS Act.*)
5. Sections 21 to 28 of the *Anti-Terrorism Act*.
6. Ibid. at 22. See sections 30 to 33 of the *CSIS Act* for specific provisions pertaining to the mandate of the Inspector General.
7. The scope and powers of review of the SIRC are set out in sections 34 to 40 of the Act.
8. R.S., 1985, c. S-7.
9. R.S.C. 1985, c. 21. This passage is a quotation from section 2 of the *RCMP Act*, which is cross-referenced in section 6 of that Act.
10. In addition to the Code provisions discussed in Chapter 1, see also the Arar Commission (2004b: 38).
11. Bill S-3, 39th Parliament - 2nd Session, 2007.
12. Section 185(1.1) and 186(1.1.) of the *Criminal Code*.
13. Section 7 of the *Anti-Terrorism Act*.
14. R.S.C. 2004, c. 15, s. 100.
15. For a more detailed discussion of the work conducted by INSETs, see the Arar Commission (2005: 5–10). The following description of inter-agency activities is derived from this document.
16. The powers of the Committee are set out in Part III of the *CSIS Act*. For a more detailed discussion of the scope and powers of the SIRC, see part D the Arar Commission (2004f).
17. The details of the following summary can be found in "Mahar Arar's Story," a document prepared by the Committee of Organizations with Intervenor Status at the Arar Commission; available at <http://www.bccla.org/temp/050509leaflet.

pdf> (last accessed February 8, 2008).

18. Press release, Arar Commission, September 18, 2006; available at <http://www.ararcommission.ca/eng/index.htm> (last accessed February 8, 2008).

19. These three men sought standing at the Arar Commission: the government of Canada successfully resisted their motion. In December of 2006, the Canadian government, under the direction of Stephen Harper, announced that a separate inquiry into the events involving these three men would be conducted by Frank Iacobucci, former Justice of the Supreme Court of Canada. A final report in the "Iacobucci Internal Inquiry" is expected in early September of 2008.

20. See "Arar's Story." The "Commissioner's ruling" referred to in this passage was rendered on December 20, 2005, and is available at <http://www.ararcommission.ca/eng/FinalrulingonnscREDACTED_Dec20.pdf> (last accessed February 8, 2008).

21. *Canada (Attorney General) v. Commission of Inquiry into the Actions of Canadian Officials in relation to Maher Arar*, 2007 FC 766.

22. R.S., 1985, c. I-11.

Conclusion

As lawmakers, judges, and law enforcers have attempted to deal, in their various ways, with the problem of terrorism since September 11th, we have witnessed a growing divide between practice and principle in the administration of justice. This was a consequence, at least in part, of a growing perception that certain departures from conventional principles have been necessary to adequately defend national security. As a result, the process of investigating and prosecuting terrorism suspects, or assessing the extent of the risk they pose to Canada, has become less fair, less transparent, and less impartial.

In the first chapter, we looked at the circumstances out of which the *Anti-Terrorism Act* had emerged. We saw that in a short period after September 11th, a majority of Parliamentarians accepted the argument that the many tools for addressing criminal behaviour in the *Criminal Code* were inadequate to counter terrorism. New terrorism offences had to be created, and new tools for the investigation and prosecution of those offences were also required. But to deal adequately with the magnitude of the threat that terrorism presented, some of these new measures would have to be innovative and arguably extreme. Although some of the measures were not altogether unprecedented in the criminal law, together they would, in fundamental ways, alter the entire process of enforcement and prosecution in the area of terrorism. Indeed, in certain respects, the complexion of the administration of justice in any area relating to national security had also been irrevocably altered.

The new offences would bring about the possibility of convicting a person for facilitating terrorism despite that person's lack of knowledge of the offence. The investigation could include the testimony of witnesses compelled to give evidence, against their will, and despite the fact that no charges had yet been laid. The prosecution of the offence could involve secret evidence, disclosed to neither the public nor the accused. The offence might also arise in part from the membership of the accused in what had been deemed a "terrorist organization," when that group was determined to be a terrorist group before having been afforded the chance to prove otherwise.

There are many examples in recent history of extraordinary measures being invoked to address extraordinary circumstances. However, what distinguishes the approach of Canada and some other western nations, including Britain, after September 11th is the view that, in the area of terrorism, extraordinary measures should form the basis of an indefinite alteration to the administration of justice. Parliamentarians in 2001 justified this view with specific reference to the *Canadian Charter of Rights and Freedoms*: they shared an implicit understanding of how extraordinary measures would be assessed in a climate of heightened fear. In short, the idea of national security had acquired a whole new resonance and importance. Activities and concerns that once seemed remote and marginal now became much less so. Measures that once would have seemed excessively cautious, even irrational, now seemed prudent and necessary.

The courts were quick to adopt the implied logic of Parliament's justification for the *Anti-Terrorism Act* and other extraordinary measures in the name of national security. Judges would find the use of security certificates to detain people indefinitely without charge, and to hold secret hearings that exclude the detainee, necessary for national security and consistent with "fundamental justice" as defined in the Charter. The courts would also find other measures consistent with the Canadian Constitution, including the use of secret evidence; the ability to deport a person to face torture; investigative hearings in which judges appear to be "allied" with the prosecution; and the possibility of convicting a person for terrorism without having to prove the act in question was intended.

The logic of necessity has become so pervasive that, in the Arar and Iacobucci inquiries, the review of the actions of both law enforcement and intelligence was seen to warrant considerable secrecy without compromising the principle of accountability. As a consequence, the Arar Commission's recommendations on how to improve the review mechanisms of the RCMP's national security activities assume uncritically that a police force can operate with the full measure of accountability when its national security activities, and the review of those activities, will be conducted mostly behind a veil of secrecy. Where this made sense in the case of CSIS, a civilian intelligence agency with limited powers and activities, it makes much less sense for a police force with a new and much broader mandate in the area of national security and terrorism. Police power is inherently more intrusive and dangerous to civil society when its exercise is unchecked. This power, coupled with the expanded scope of state secrecy in national security, comes very close to power without accountability.

In these various ways, developments in counter-terrorism have widened a gap within the administration of justice between its guiding principles and their practical application. At the outset of this study, I cited the work of Gillian Balfour, Elizabeth Comack, and Ngaire Naffine, to help frame my analysis in terms of a broader understanding of the relationship between the discourse or ideology of the law and the practical world in which it unfolds. Recalling that discussion, Balfour and Comack take the view that a divide has always existed between the ideals to which the legal system purports to subscribe, and the practical workings and actual effects of that system (2004: 10). They draw upon Naffine's analysis of the fallacies entailed by what Naffine has called the "Official Version of Law" (1990). This is a version of the law that was discernable in the government's rhetoric when introducing the *Anti-Terrorism Act* in Parliament. Then Minister of Justice Anne McLellan claimed the Act to be consistent with Charter rights and values: she suggested that its proposed amendments would address terrorism in a way that maintained the fair, just, and dispassionate character of the law. The "Official Version" can also be traced in the opinions of various judges who find certain counter-terror measures consistent with conventional principles that include impartiality, procedural fairness, and fundamental justice. We can also see this version of law's ideology at work in the Arar and Iacobucci inquiries, where the judge believed that the process of holding hearings served accountability despite the fact of their being held under so much secrecy.

For Naffine, the Official Version of Law rests on two fallacies: both of these can be better understood by looking at the recent impact of terrorism on the administration of justice. The legal system assumes that it is possible to create, apply, and enforce law in a manner that is purely dispassionate, universal, and non-ideological. It also assumes that the subject of the law is a person whom the law can approach while remaining blind to his or her qualities. But in practice, neither of these assumptions is tenable. Ideology and specific historical and cultural conditions affect the way law operates on every level, including our approach to subject of the law.

Counter-terror initiatives in Canada after September 11th have provided ample evidence of this. The *Anti-Terrorism Act*, a law crafted around the figure of the terrorist, assumes a fundamental distinction between a normal criminal subject — who is afforded the full range of due process protections — and a subject to whom we can afford to extend only some of these protections, or many of them with significant modifications. Not all criminal subjects, in other words, are the same. The application of anti-terror law and policy in the sphere of immigration calls into question the universality of the presumption of innocence when it leads to indefinite detentions without charge; it raises doubts about the degree of disinterest on the part of a court that works closely with the prosecution to decide on disclosure; and it invites suspicion about ideological trappings when it proves itself quick to condemn on the basis of information purporting to connect a suspect with Islamic extremism. With Balfour and Comack we might go a step further and point to ways in which counter-terror law and policy, like other areas of the law, have reproduced social stereotypes and inequalities. Despite much that has been said about the dangers of profiling in the context of counter-terrorism, a number of submissions by advocacy groups to Parliamentary committees in 2001, including the three-year review of the *Anti-Terrorism Act*, attested to the fact that two groups of Canadians, which sometimes overlap — Muslims and those of Arab descent — have been affected differently and disproportionately by counter-terror law and policy. The experiences of Maher Arar, Abdullah Almalki, Ahmad Abou El-Maati, and Muayyed Nureddin in relation to Canadian officials suggest that ideological fears and prejudices play at least some part in the practice of counter-terrorism.

If we can assume, then, with Naffine, Comack, and Balfour, that law always functions at a remove from its own ideals, and that it should be situated somewhere apart from the letter of the law, how can we account for the growing gap between practice and principle in anti-terrorism procedures? Perhaps the most decisive aspect of this gap, the very source of its growth since 2001, is an argument that many have accepted uncritically: that we are inadequately equipped for the threat of terrorism unless we resort to unusual measures. And perhaps the most significant measure perceived to be necessary is that the state must now function with far greater secrecy than ever before. If this means less disclosure to accused persons, more secret trials, more secret inquiries, more secret reports, then so be it.

We might begin to account for this logic by approaching it as a product of a specific historical and cultural belief. In other words, in a climate of heightened fear, many lawmakers, judges, law enforcers, and members of the intelligence community have not sought to justify the need for certain measures, but have instead sought to justify certain measures as necessary. Some commentators, including Kent Roach and Ziyaad Mia, have questioned the necessity for new criminal law measures to deal adequately with the threat of terrorism. As noted in the first chapter, Mia has argued that the *Criminal Code* already included a range of tools that could be used to prevent future acts of terrorism, including the conspiracy provisions, as well as those allowing for conditions under a "peace bond" or recognizance, where there are reasonable grounds to believe an offence may be committed. The Code also included a number of offences involving violence to persons or to property that were perfectly adequate for holding people (or groups of people) accountable for terrorist acts. The accused in the Air India bombing, for example, were prosecuted by way of a multi-count indictment for conspiracy to endanger the safety of persons on an airplane, and for murder.

How were these offences, already delineated in the Code, inadequate to address the most infamous terrorism case in Canadian history? Kent Roach has encapsulated this argument by suggesting that "the failure of September 11 was one of law enforcement, not of the criminal law" (2003: 23).

A similar argument applies to the apparent need for greater secrecy. Before 2001, the court could invoke provisions in the *Canada Evidence Act* to protect any information in respect to which "disclosure would be injurious to... international relations or national defence or security." (It now allows for the protection of any information that is "potentially injurious," and also any information relating to national security that the government is "taking measures to safeguard.") The older version clearly expresses a rationale for keeping information secret, and it contains a clear test. The question is what further protection is gained by blurring the line between injurious and potentially injurious, or erasing it altogether in favour of secrecy for any information the government wishes to safeguard? In other words, if the court finds that disclosure would not be injurious to national security, why should the information be kept secret? What was wrong with the old test? The government simply assumed its inadequacy without demonstrating it.

Revisiting these questions and asking whether we are in fact better protected by the *Anti-Terrorism Act*, and related measures, brings us closer to narrowing the gap between principle and practice in the administration of justice. Although there will always be a divide between theory and practice, or between the Official Version of the Law and the reality we encounter, there are measures in the present legislation that widen this gap, while proving to be neither as necessary nor as helpful as some have argued. If we repealed the *Anti-Terrorism Act*, returned to the earlier test for privilege in the *Canada Evidence Act*, and included measures for a fairer process for detainees in security certificate cases, our criminal justice system and immigration law would be more humane, more respectful of basic democratic values, and no less effective in protecting us.

Avenues for Change

There are a number of other avenues to bring about change in anti-terrorism law and practice, including influencing public opinion, Parliament, and the courts, as well as reviewing the policies and practices of law enforcement and those in the intelligence community.

The law and policy discussed in this book will not likely change, however, without a shift in public attitudes and priorities with respect to criminal justice, immigration, and counter-terrorism law itself. We have some indication of where the public stands, or stood relatively recently, on the measures taken by the government in 2001, and can use this information to assess work that might be done to raise public awareness of the issues. A pair of studies was conducted for the Department of Justice in the winter of 2004.[1] The first study canvassed the views of 196 people in twenty-two focus groups held in Toronto, Ottawa, Winnipeg, Montreal, Calgary, Regina, Vancouver, Quebec City, and Halifax. The participants were aged eighteen and over. The report concluded:

> Awareness of the anti-terrorism legislation was generally low, with about only half of the participants in each group saying, when prompted, that they were aware of some aspects of the legislation. There was also low recall of pre-9/11 Canadian terrorist incidents; post-9/11 terrorist incidents outside of Canada were mentioned more often. The general feeling was that terrorist incidents in Canada prior to September 11, 2001, would have been dealt with under the *Criminal Code*; however, there was uncertainty as to what aspect of the Code would apply to terrorism. Participants were generally aware of heightened airport and border security measures, as well as tougher immigration procedures post-9/11....
>
> Overall, participants felt that the risks associated with the *Anti-Terrorism Act* and the new powers it bestows on the police were acceptable in light of the protection the Act affords to the country and its citizens, although the level of safety they felt did not change after learning about the provisions of the Act, since they did not feel unsafe to begin with. The majority of participants said that the Act has had no direct impact on them, apart from them having to wait longer at the border or in line for ticketing or security at airports, which can primarily be attributed to post-9/11 security measures rather than to the Act itself. A few participants stated that they had friends or relatives adversely affected by post September 11 security measures, with experiences ranging from being pulled over at the border to being deported from the United States. In these cases, the individuals affected were said to be members of visible minority groups.[2]

The views of members of minority groups formed the object of the second study, which was conducted by the Research and Statistics division of the Department of Justice.[3] In that study, "[sixteen] focus groups were carried out in Halifax, Montreal, Toronto, Calgary, and Vancouver covering 138 male and female participants from approximately 60 ethno-cultural minority backgrounds."[4] The report concluded:

> Overall, participants expressed general support for the provisions of the *Anti-Terrorism Act*, with varying degrees of concern about its

application. The Act was generally thought to create a sense of comfort, safety, and increased security. Participants generally assumed that Canada's anti-terrorism legislation was less severe than that of the United States and the United Kingdom....

Overall, the majority of focus group participants felt the risk of having the [*Anti-Terrorism Act*] and its new police powers were acceptable to protect the country and its population. Most felt safer or the same with the legislation, and most hoped their reservations would not be validated. People adopted a "wait-and-see" approach.[5]

Public opinion may have evolved since these surveys were taken. But they still provide a helpful snapshot of majority and minority views of the Act at an early stage in its history, and certain points can be gleaned.

The two surveys suggest a number of common features in the two groups. The members of both groups appear unaware of the specifics of the *Anti-Terrorism Act*, and both are deferential to Parliament's decision to bring about the Act — findings that would likely be true today. Perhaps most significantly, members of both groups believe the risks entailed in granting police more power were acceptable in light of the goal of protecting Canada. Notably, after learning more about the content of the Act, most of those in the general survey group did not believe the Act affected their level of safety, whereas most of those in the survey of members of minority groups believed that it did.

The survey asked whether anti-terror legislation, with its increase in police powers, was acceptable. It did not ask whether the legislation, or any increase in powers, was necessary. We can infer from these surveys something between a measure of indifference on the part of the public and a measure of acceptance. We cannot be sure the wider public would concur with the proposition that extraordinary measures are necessary for an adequate response to terrorism. But the public's acquiescence in the steps taken by Parliament and the courts in this direction are crucial. Whether the public will continue to acquiesce is another issue.

For a brief span of time, in early 2007, the subject of the *Anti-Terrorism Act* returned to public consciousness as Parliament debated the merits of extending the preventive arrest and investigative hearing provisions. It was a shallow and deeply partisan debate, which Kent Roach has described as "dismal." The government, as Roach noted, "accused the opposition of being unsympathetic to the victims of terrorism. The opposition accused the government of engaging in slurs. What got lost in all this partisan bickering was reasonable discussion of the merits of the two controversial provisions that expired" (2007b).

Since then, there has been some public discussion about the committee reports on the (delayed) three-year Parliamentary review of the Act and some public discussion of the amendments to the security certificate regime in February of 2008: there will continue to be debate in certain quarters as to the merits and necessity of extraordinary measures in the field of counter-terrorism.

However, the hope for real change lies in a public that is better informed, no longer indifferent, and, ideally, mobilized for change. We might envision a more concerned public that places pressure on lawmakers, law enforcement and other stakeholders in the national security field to amend law and practices that are thought to be unfair and inhumane. This process could begin with more involvement from all of the stakeholders in the system, including the communities most directly affected by the practical injustices of counter-terror law and policy. Those in the position to shape the law directly — members of the government and of the judiciary — will also need to become better attuned to the many different concerns at issue in this debate.

Another way in which public opinion might be mobilized is through more exposure to cases like those of Arar, Almalki, Abou-Elmaati, Nureddin, and the "secret trial five." One exemplary initiative in this respect was an event called "Measuring Security Measures" (2005) produced by Citizenshift, an organization affiliated with the National Film Board of Canada, together with a community organization called Überculture. The event was staged in a number of cities across Canada and consisted of an evening in which members of the public were invited to view a series of short documentary films dealing with the plight of security certificate detainees and their families, and the effect of other national security measures on both citizens and non-citizens alike. Producers of the films were on hand for discussion, along with activists, lawyers, scholars, and others. This initiative, and other serious media and academic attention to the issues, points us in the direction of a greater awareness and level of engagement in the debate about counter-terrorism.

But a change in public opinion will not, in itself, bridge the gap between practice and principle in the administration of justice. Ultimately, policy makers, legislators, judges, and members of law enforcement and intelligence will have to abandon the logic that dictates the necessity for extraordinary measures or greater secrecy as the only effective way of protecting national security. This will certainly involve more public discussion of the issues, more research, and more education. But it will also help to realize that the more we step back and ask what it is we wish to protect, the more secure we will be.

Notes

1. Millward Brown Goldfarb, "Public Views on the *Anti-Terrorism Act* (Formerly Bill C-36); a Qualitative Study." See <http://www.justice.gc.ca/en/ps/rs/rep/2005/rr05-3/index.html> (last accessed January 9, 2007).
2. Ibid.
3. "Minority Views on the Canadian Anti-Terrorism Act (Formerly Bill C-36) A Qualitative Study." See <http://www.justice.gc.ca/en/anti_terr/reports.html> (last accessed January 9, 2007).
4. Ibid.
5. Ibid., p. 2.

References

Agamben, Giorgio. 2005. *State of Exception*. Chicago: University of Chicago Press.

Ahmed, Kamal, and A. Barnet. 2001. "Britain Placed Under State of Emergency." *The Observer*, November 11.

Arar Commission (of Inquiry into the Actions of Canadian Officials in Relation to Maher Arar). 2004a. "Accountability and Transparency." Ottawa: Arar Commission.

_____. 2004b. "The RCMP and National Security." Ottawa: Arar Commission.

_____. 2004c. "Police Independence." Ottawa: Arar Commission.

_____. 2004d. "Domestic Models of Review of Police Forces." Ottawa: Arar Commission.

_____. 2004e. "Consultation Paper." Ottawa: Arar Commission (October 5).

_____. 2004f. "Accountability of Security Intelligence in Canada." Ottawa: Arar Commission.

_____. 2005. "The RCMP and National Security: Supplementary Background Paper." Ottawa: Arar Commission.

_____. 2006a. "Report of the Events Relating to Maher Arar: Analysis and Recommendations." Ottawa: Arar Commission.

_____. 2006b. "Report of the Events Relating to Maher Arar: Factual Background." Ottawa: Arar Commission.

_____. 2006c. "A New Review Mechanism for the RCMP's National Security Activities." Ottawa: Arar Commission.

_____. 2007. "Press Release: Arar Commission discloses more information to the public." Ottawa: Arar Commission.

Arar, Maher. 2008. "Maher's Story." Available at <http://www.maherarar.ca/mahers%20story.php> (last accessed June 2008).

British Columbia Civil Liberties Association. 2005. "National Security: Curbing the Excess to Protect Freedom and Democracy." Vancouver: British Columbia Civil Liberties Association.

Canada, Department of Justice. 2004. "Minority Views on the Canadian Anti-Terrorism Act (Formerly Bill C-36) A Qualitative Study." Ottawa: Department of Justice.

_____. 2007. "Response of the Government of Canada to the Final Report of the Standing Committee on Public Safety and National Security Subcommittee on the Review of the *Anti-Terrorism Act.*" Ottawa: Department of Justice.

Canada, Minister of Supply and Services. 1981. *Report of the Royal Commission on Security.* Ottawa: Minister of Supply and Services Canada.

Carver, Peter. 2002. "Shelter from the Storm: A Comment on *Suresh v. Canada (Minister of Citizenship and Immigration).*" *Alberta Law Review* 10, 465.

CAUT (Canadian Association of University Teachers). 2005. *Submission to the House of Commons Subcommittee on Public Safety and National Security Regarding the Review of the Anti-Terrorism Act.* Ottawa: Canadian Association of University Teachers.

Comack, Elizabeth, and G. Balfour. 2004. *The Power to Criminalize: Violence, Inequality and the Law.* Halifax: Fernwood.

_____. 2006. "Introduction." In E. Comack (ed.), *Locating Law: Race/Class/Gender Connections.* Halifax: Fernwood.

Commission of Inquiry Concerning Certain Activities of the Royal Canadian Mounted Police. (McDonald Commission) 1981. "Second Report: Freedom and Security Under the Law." Ottawa: Supply and Services Canada.

Committee of Organizations with Intervenor Status at the Arar Inquiry. 2005. "Mahar Arar's Story." Ottawa Committee of Organizations with Intervenor Status at the Arar Inquiry.

Cotler, Irwin. 2001. "Thinking Outside of the Box: Foundational Principles for a Counter-Terrorism Law and Policy." In R. Daniels and P. Macklem (eds.), *The Security of Freedom: Essays on Canada's Anti-Terrorism Bill.* Toronto: University of Toronto Press.

_____. 2003. "Terrorism, Security and Rights: The Dilemma of Democracies." *National Journal of Constitutional Law* 14, 13.

Dicey, A.V. 1965. *Introduction to the Law of the Constitution.* London: MacMillan and Co.

Dworkin, Ronald. 1977. *Taking Rights Seriously.* Cambridge: Harvard University Press.

_____. 2002. "The Threat to Patriotism." *New York Review of Books* 49, 3 (February).

_____. 2003. "Terror and the Attack on Civil Liberties." *New York Review of Books* 50, 17 (November).

_____. 2004. "What the Court Really Said." *New York Review of Books* 51, 13 (August).

Dyzenhaus, David. 2001. "The Permanence of the Temporary." In R. Daniels and P. Macklem (eds.), *The Security of Freedom: Essays on Canada's Anti-Terrorism Bill.* Toronto: University of Toronto Press.

Forcese, Craig. 2008. "Is Bill C-3 the Security Way to Go?" *The Globe and Mail,* February 6.

Freeze, Colin. 2007. "Crown Calls for Video Monitoring of Terrorism Suspect." *Globe and Mail,* October 30: A1

Goldfarb, Millward Brown. 2004. "Public Views on the Anti-Terrorism Act: A Qualitative Study." Available at <http://www.justice.gc.ca/en/anti_terr/reports/html> (accessed January 9, 2007). Ottawa, Department of Justice.

Grant, Kathy. 2003. "The Unjust Impact of Canada's *Anti-Terrorism Act* on an Accused's Right to Full Answer and Defence." *Windsor Review of Legal and Social Issues* 16, 137.

Heafey, Shirley. 2002. "Civilian Oversight in a Changed World." Ottawa: Commission for Public Complaints Against the RCMP.

Mia, Ziyaad. 2003. "Terrorizing the Rule of Law: Implications of the *Anti-Terrorism Act*." *National Journal of Constitutional Law* 14, 126.

Naffine, Ngaire. 1990. *The Law and the Sexes: Explorations in Feminist Jurisprudence.* Sydney: Allen and Unwin.

Peppin, Patricia. 1993. "Emergency Legislation and Rights in Canada: The War Measures Act and Civil Liberties." *Queen's Law Journal* 18, 129.

Pue, W. Wesley. 2003. "The War on Terror: Constitutional Governance in a State of Perpetual Warfare." *Osgoode Hall Law Journal* 41, 267.

Roach, Kent. 2001. "Dangers of a Charter-Proof and Crime-Based Response to Terrorism." In R. Daniels and P. Macklem (eds.), *The Security of Freedom: Essays on Canada's Anti-Terrorism Bill.* Toronto: University of Toronto Press.

_____. 2001. "The New Terrorism Offences and the Criminal Law." In R. Daniels and P. Macklem (eds.), *The Security of Freedom: Essays on Canada's Anti-Terrorism Bill.* Toronto: University of Toronto Press.

_____. 2002. "Canadian Values in the Face of Terrorism." *McGill Law Journal* 47, 4.

_____. 2002. "Did September 11 Change Everything? Struggling to Preserve Canadian Values in the Face of Terrorism." *McGill Law Journal* 47, 893.

_____. 2003. *September 11: Consequences for Canada.* Montreal: McGill-Queens University Press.

_____. 2006. "Canadian Anti-Terror Law on Trial: The Toronto Terrorism Arrests." *Jurist,* June 10.

_____. 2007a. "Better Late Than Never: the Canadian Parliamentary Review of the *Anti-Terrorism Act*." *Choices* 13, 5. Montreal: Institute for Research on Public Policy.

_____. 2007b. "Canada's New Terrorism Bills: Slow Down and Debate." *Jurist,* October 29. Available at <http://jurist.law.pitt.edu/forumy/2007/10/canadas-new-terrorism-bills-slow-down.php> (accessed on May 25, 2008).

Roach, Kent, and G. Trotter. 2005. "Miscarriages of Justice in the War Against Terror." 109 *Penn State Law Review* 109, 967.

Rosenthal, Peter. 2003. "Disclosure to the Defence after September 11: Sections 37 and 38 of the *Canada Evidence Act*." *Criminal Law Quarterly* 48, 186.

Royal Commission on Security. 1969. "Report of the Royal Commission on Security." (McKenzie Commission) Ottawa: Queen's Printer.

Schneiderman, David, and Brenda Cossman. 2001. "Political Association and the Anti-Terrorism Bill." In R. Daniels and P. Macklem (eds.), *The Security of Freedom: Essays on Canada's Anti-Terrorism Bill.* Toronto: University of Toronto Press.

Schwartz, Bernard. 1977. *The Great Rights of Mankind: A History of the American Bill of Rights.* New York: Oxford University Press.

Shaffer, Martha. 2001. "Effectiveness of Anti-Terrorism Legislation: Does Bill C-36 Give Us What We Need?" In R. Daniels and P. Macklem (eds.), *The Security of Freedom: Essays on Canada's Anti-Terrorism Bill.* Toronto: University of Toronto

Press.

Stewart, Hamish. 2001. "Rule of Law or Executive Fiat? Bill C-36 and Public Interest Immunity." In R. Daniels and P. Macklem (eds.), *The Security of Freedom: Essays on Canada's Anti-Terrorism Bill*. Toronto: University of Toronto Press.

_____. 2003. "Public Interest Immunity after Bill C-36." *Criminal Law Quarterly* 47, 249.

Stuart, Don. 2003. "The Anti-Terrorism Bill C-36: An Unnecessary Law and Order Quick Fix That Permanently Stains the Canadian Criminal Justice System." *National Journal of Constitutional Law* 14, 153.

Walkham, Thomas. 2007. "Secrecy Threatens Credibility of Iacobucci Inquiry." *Toronto Star*, October 18.

Weinrib, Lorraine. 2001. "Terrorism's Challenge to the Constitutional Order." In R. Daniels and P. Macklem (eds.), *The Security of Freedom: Essays on Canada's Anti-Terrorism Bill*. Toronto: University of Toronto Press.

Legislation and Conventions

Anti-Terrorism Act, S.C. 2001, c. 41.

Anti-Terrorism, Crime and Security Act, 2001, Acts of the U.K. Parliament, 2001, c. 24.

Canada Evidence Act, R.S.C. 1985, c. C-5.

Canadian Charter of Rights and Freedoms, Part I of the *Constitution Act, 1982*, being Schedule B to the *Canada Act 1982* (U.K.), 1982, c. 11.

Canadian Security Intelligence Service Act, R.S.C. 1985 c. C-23.

Constitution Act, 1867 (U.K.), 30 & 31 Vict., c. 3, reprinted in R.S.C. 1985, App. II, No. 5.

Constitution Act, 1982, being Schedule B to the *Canada Act 1982* (U.K.), 1982, c. 11.

Convention for the Protection of Human Rights and Fundamental Freedoms, as amended by Protocol No. 11, Council of Europe, Rome, 4. XI. 1950.

Criminal Code, R.S. 1985, c. C-46.

Emergencies Act, S.C. 1988, c. 29

European Convention for the Protection of Human Rights and Fundamental Freedoms (1950) 213 U.N.T.S. 221.

Extradition Act, R.S.C. 1985, c. E-23.

Geneva Convention Relative to the Treatment of Prisoners of War (1949) Can. T.S. 1965 No. 20.

Immigration Act, R.S.C. 1985, c. 1-2.

Immigration and Refugee Protection Act, S.C. 2001, c-27

Inquiries Act, R.S., c. I-13, s.1.

Intelligence Services Act (U.K.), 1994, c. 13.

International Covenant on Civil and Political Rights (1966) Can. T.S. 1976 No. 47.

National Defence Act, R.S., 1985, c. N-5.

Prevention of Terrorism Act, 2005, Acts of the U.K. Parliament, c. 2.

Proceeds of Crime (Money Laundering) and Terrorist Financing Act, S.C. 2000, c. 17.

Public Safety Act, 2002, S.C. 2004, c. 15.

Royal Canadian Mounted Police Act, R.S., 1985, c. R-10.

Security Offences Act, R.S., 1985, c. S-7.

Terrorism Act, 2000, Acts of the U.K. Parliament, 2000, c. 11.

Uniting and Strengthening America by Providing Appropriate Tools Required To Intercept and

Obstruct Terrorism (USA PATRIOT) Act of 2001, Pub. L. No. 107-56, 115 Stat. 272, 276 (2001).
Universal Declaration of Human Rights (1948) GA Res. 217 A (III), U.N. Doc. A/810.
War Measures Act, S.C, 1914, c. 2.

Jurisprudence:
A (FC) and Others (FC) v. SSHD, [2004] UKHL 56.
Ahani v. Canada (Minister of Citizenship and Immigration), [2002] 1 S.C.R. 72.
Almrei v. Canada (Minister of Citizenship and Immigration), 2005 FCA 54.
Canada (Attorney General) v. Commission of Inquiry into the Actions of Canadian Officials in relation to Maher Arar, 2007 FC 766.
Canada (Minister of Citizenship and Immigration) v. Jaballah, 1999 F.C.J. No. 1681.
Canada (Minister of Citizenship and Immigration) v. Mahjoub, 2004 FC 1028.
Canada (Minister of Citizenship and Immigration) v. Mahjoub (T.D.), 2001 FCT 1095, [2001] 4 F.C. 644.
Charkaoui (Re) 2004 FCA 421.
Charkaoui v. Canada (Citizenship and Immigration), [2007] 1 S.C.R. 350, 2007 SCC 9.
Baker v. Canada (Minister of Citizenship and Immigration), [1999] 2 S.C.R. 817.
Blencoe v. British Columbia (Human Rights Commission), [2000] 2 S.C.R. 307.
British Columbia v. Imperial Tobacco Canada Ltd., 2005 SCC 49.
Hat'm Abu Zayda v. Israel General Security Service, 38 I.L.M. 1471 (1999).
Hamdan v. Rumsfeld, 548 U.S. (2006).
Hamdi v. Rumsfeld, 542 U.S. 507 (2004).
Harkat v. Canada (Minister of Citizenship and Immigration), [2004] F.C.J. No. 1104.
Hunter v. Southam, (1984) 14 C.C.C. (3) 97.
Kindler v. Canada (Minister of Justice), [1991] 2 S.C.R. 779.
Law v. Canada (Minister of Employment and Immigration), [1999] 1 S.C.R. 497.
R. v. Khawaja, [2006] C.C.S. No. 12212, [2006] O.J. No. 4245.
R. v. Malik and Bagri, 2005 BCSC 350.
R. v. Malmo-Levine; R. v. Caine, [2003] 3 S.C.R. 571.
R. v. Mills, [1999] 3 S.C.R. 668.
R. v. Nova Scotia Pharmaceutical Society, [1992] 2 S.C.R. 606.
R. v. O'Connor, [1995] 4 S.C.R. 411.
R. v. Oakes, [1986] 1 S.C.R. 103.
Rasul v. Bush, 542 U.S. 466 (2004).
Re Application Under s. 83.28 of the Criminal Code, [2004] 2 S.C.R. 248.
Re B.C. Motor Vehicle Act, [1985] 2 S.C.R. 486.
Re Charkaoui, 2005 FC 248.
Re Jaballah, 2005 FC 399.
Re Vancouver Sun, [2004] 2 S.C.R. 332.
Reference re Ng Extradition (Can.), [1991] 2 S.C.R. 858.
Rodriguez v. British Columbia (Attorney General), [1993] 3 S.C.R. 519.
Saygili v. Canada (Minister of Citizenship & Immigration), (1997) 127 F.T.C.R. 112.
Secretary of State for the Home Department v. Rehman, [2001] 3 W.L.R. 877.
Suresh v. Canada (Minister of Citizenship and Immigration), [2002] 1 S.C.R. 3.
Toronto Star v. Canada, [2007] F.C. 128.
United States v. Burns, [2001] 1 S.C.R. 283.